总主编 文 旭

NEW WORLD
INTERACTIVE ENGLISH

新世界

交互英语 视听说 3 学生用书

主　编：李成坚
副主编：易　红　宋　冰
编　者：（按姓氏笔画顺序）
　　　　王　焰　孙　颖　李　捷
　　　　迟维佳　金　艾

原版主编：Rob Jenkins
原版作者：Kristin L. Johannsen
　　　　　Rebecca Tarver Chase

清華大学出版社
北 京

Copyright © 2017 by National Geographic Learning, a Cengage company.
Original edition published by Cengage Learning. All Rights reserved.
本书原版由圣智学习出版公司出版。版权所有，盗印必究。

Tsinghua University Press is authorized by Cengage Learning to publish and distribute exclusively this adaptation edition. This edition is authorized for sale in the People's Republic of China only (excluding Hong Kong SAR, Macao SAR and Taiwan). Unauthorized export of this edition is a violation of the Copyright Act. No part of this publication may be reproduced or distributed by any means, or stored in a database or retrieval system, without the prior written permission of the publisher.
本改编版由圣智学习出版公司授权清华大学出版社独家出版发行。此版本仅限在中华人民共和国境内（不包括中国香港、澳门特别行政区及中国台湾）销售。未经授权的本书出口将被视为违反版权法的行为。未经出版者预先书面许可，不得以任何方式复制或发行本书的任何部分。

"National Geographic", "National Geographic Society" and the Yellow Border Design are registered trademarks of the National Geographic Society® Marcas Registradas.

Cengage Learning Asia Pte. Ltd.
151 Lorong Chuan, #02-08 New Tech Park, Singapore 556741
本书封面贴有 Cengage Learning 防伪标签，无标签者不得销售。

北京市版权局著作权合同登记号　图字：01-2016-8549

版权所有，侵权必究。侵权举报电话：010-62782989 13701121933

图书在版编目（CIP）数据

新世界交互英语. 视听说学生用书. 3 / 文旭总主编；李成坚主编. —北京：清华大学出版社，2017（2017.7重印）
ISBN 978-7-302-46297-2

Ⅰ.①新… Ⅱ.①文… ②李… Ⅲ.①英语—听说教学—高等学校—教材 Ⅳ.①H319.39

中国版本图书馆 CIP 数据核字（2017）第 021492 号

责任编辑：蔡心奕
封面设计：平　原
责任校对：王凤芝
责任印制：王静怡

出版发行：清华大学出版社
　　网　　址：http://www.tup.com.cn, http://www.wqbook.com
　　地　　址：北京清华大学学研大厦 A 座　　邮　编：100084
　　社 总 机：010-62770175　　邮　购：010-62786544
　　投稿与读者服务：010-62776969, c-service@tup.tsinghua.edu.cn
　　质 量 反 馈：010-62772015, zhiliang@tup.tsinghua.edu.cn
印 装 者：北京盛通印刷股份有限公司
经　　销：全国新华书店
开　　本：210mm×285mm　　印　张：8.75　　字　数：246千字
版　　次：2017年3月第1版　　印　次：2017年7月第2次印刷
定　　价：49.00元

产品编号：071817-01

PREFACE

《国家中长期教育改革和发展规划纲要（2010–2020年）》明确指出，要"适应国家经济社会对外开放的要求，培养大批具有国际视野、通晓国际规则、能够参与国际事务和国际竞争的国际化人才"。《大学英语教学指南》提出，"大学英语课程应根据本科专业类教学质量国家标准，参照本指南进行合理定位，服务于学校的办学目标、院系人才培养的目标和学生个性化发展的需求"。

《新世界交互英语》是清华大学出版社站在国家外语教育与人才培养的战略高度，从美国圣智学习出版公司引进优质原版素材、精心打造出版的一套通用大学英语教材。为满足国内大学英语教学的实际需要，出版社邀请国内多所大学，在《大学英语教学指南》的指导下，对原版教材进行了改编。本套教材汇集全球顶尖品牌教学资源，贯彻启发性教学理念，以课堂教学为纽带，将全球化视野与学生真实生活联系起来，注重学生个性化发展需求，力求培养具有较高英语应用能力和跨文化交际能力的国际化人才。

一、教材特色

本套教材主要有以下特色：

❶ 素材来源：汇集全球顶尖品牌教学资源

本套教材的素材源自全球两大顶尖品牌教学资源：美国国家地理（National Geographic Learning）和TED演讲（TED Talks），为学生提供了大量原汁原味的视频、音频和图片*，将世界各地的自然风光、风土人情、文化习俗带进课堂，以拓展学生的思维，并拓宽他们的国际化视野，从而达到提高学生语言应用能力和跨文化交际能力之目的。

❷ 编写理念：倡导启发性教学

本套教材将全球真实事件和精彩观点引入教学，结合中国传统文化和国情，注重思维训练，启发思考，以帮助学生理解中西文化差异，在培养学生听说读写译等英语应用能力的同时，着力培养其国际视野和创新精神，实现学生的全面发展。

❸ 核心目标：用课堂连接世界与学生生活

本套教材以课堂教学为纽带，将多姿多彩的世界万象与触手可及的学生生活连接起来，让学生具有全球化视野的同时，关注自身生活，思考中国问题，并学会用英语去表达自己的思想，从而成长为兼具扎实英语基本功和敏锐批判性思维的国际化人才。

---

*本教材配套的视、音频资源，请登录www.tsinghuawaiyu.com，"点击进入"清华外语数字化学习平台，登录平台之后，到"公共资源"中下载。

PREFACE

二、改编思路

中方编写团队在对原版教材进行本土化改编过程中,做了适当的增补、替换和删减等工作。主要改编思路如下:

❶ 增补中国文化和中国国情内容

本教材注重培养学生对中国传统文化的认同,着力培养学生使用英语介绍中国文化的能力。在问题设计、练习改编方面重视本土问题,以帮助学生理解中西文化差异;在翻译、写作、口语活动中融入文化对比的元素,启迪学生对本土文化进行思考,培养其国际视野和中国情怀。

❷ 设计实用型和兴趣型练习

在设计练习时,适当参考了雅思、托福、大学英语四六级考试的题型,补充了更多的听力、翻译等练习,增强了教材的实用性;同时,结合时代发展,我们在"读写译"系列中加入扫描二维码以获取更多主题阅读材料的新元素,以充分调动学生的学习兴趣和求知欲望,使他们在主动学习的过程中提高英语水平和综合素养。

❸ 引入批判性思维训练和创新写作题型

本教材注重引导学生正确区分人物与观点、事实与解释、审美与判断、语言与现实、字面义与隐含义等,对问题进行批判性评价。"读写译"系列教材每个单元专门设计了一项针对批判性思维训练的练习,根据阅读模块内容启迪学生深度思考,进而提出独到见解;在写作能力培养上,设计了环环相扣、逻辑紧密的练习,体裁题材多样,积极鼓励创新写作,实现批判思维与创新写作的结合。

三、教材结构

本套教材分为"视听说"和"读写译"两个独立系列,每个系列包含学生用书和教师用书各四个级别。每个级别包含八个单元,每个单元可供四课时使用。

其中,"视听说"每个单元包含两大部分。第一部分主要围绕音频素材展开,包含A、B、C、D四个板块,分别对应四个教学目标(Goals)。第二部分的E、F两个板块主要包括视频素材和拓展练习,每个单元均包含美国国家地理录像视频Video Journal和拓展练习Further Practice,每两个单元之后含一个TED Talks视频。

"读写译"每个单元包含Reading、Writing和Translation三个部分。Reading部分包含两篇课文，Writing部分介绍若干个Writing Skills，Translation部分包含汉译英和英译汉两个篇章翻译练习。每个单元最后都设计了Weaving It Together综合和拓展板块，用以培养学生课下自学能力。

四、适用对象

本套教材适用于我国大学公共英语教学，也适用于成人自学。

五、编写团队

本套教材的总主编为西南大学文旭教授。"视听说"1–4册主编分别为：西南大学莫启扬、西南石油大学孙阳、西南交通大学李成坚、内蒙古大学段满福；"读写译"1–4册主编分别为：山东大学崔校平、哈尔滨理工大学姜毓锋、贵州师范大学刘瑾、西安电子科技大学马刚。来自全国近十所高校的几十名专家和骨干教师参与了本套教材的设计和编写，美国圣智学习出版公司的英语教育专家和教材编写专家对全书进行了审定。

在改编之前，我们广泛咨询了国内外英语教育领域的资深专家学者，开展了充分的调研和分析，确定了本套教材的改编理念和方案，最终使本套教材得以与广大师生见面。教材的改编凝聚了诸多专家学者的经验和智慧。在此，对为本套教材的改编和出版付出辛勤劳动的所有老师以及出版社的各位同仁表示衷心的感谢。由于水平有限，不足之处在所难免。我们真诚地希望大家提出宝贵意见，并在未来的修订中使之更趋完善。

文旭

2017年2月

UNIT WALK-THROUGH

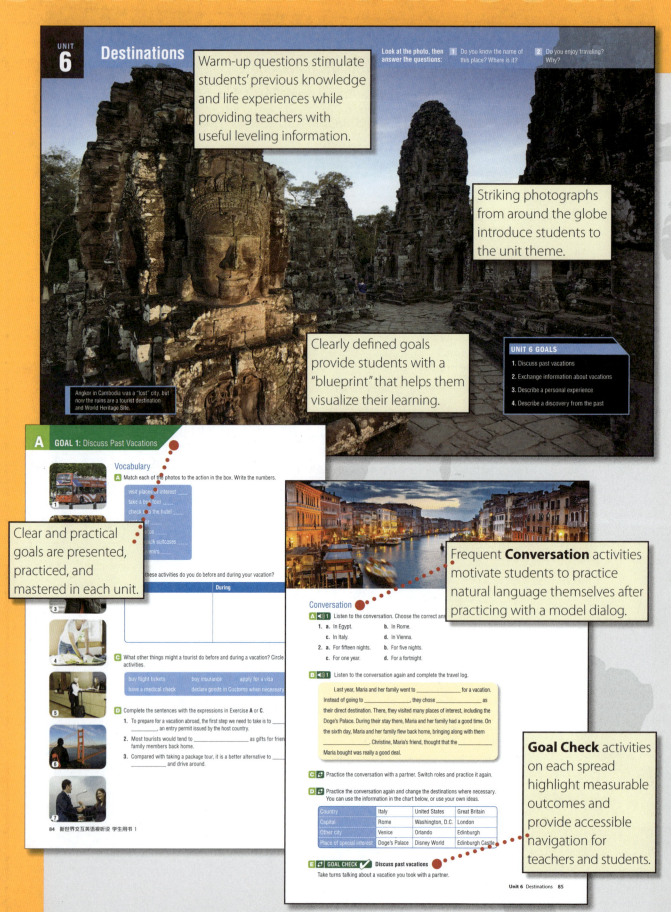

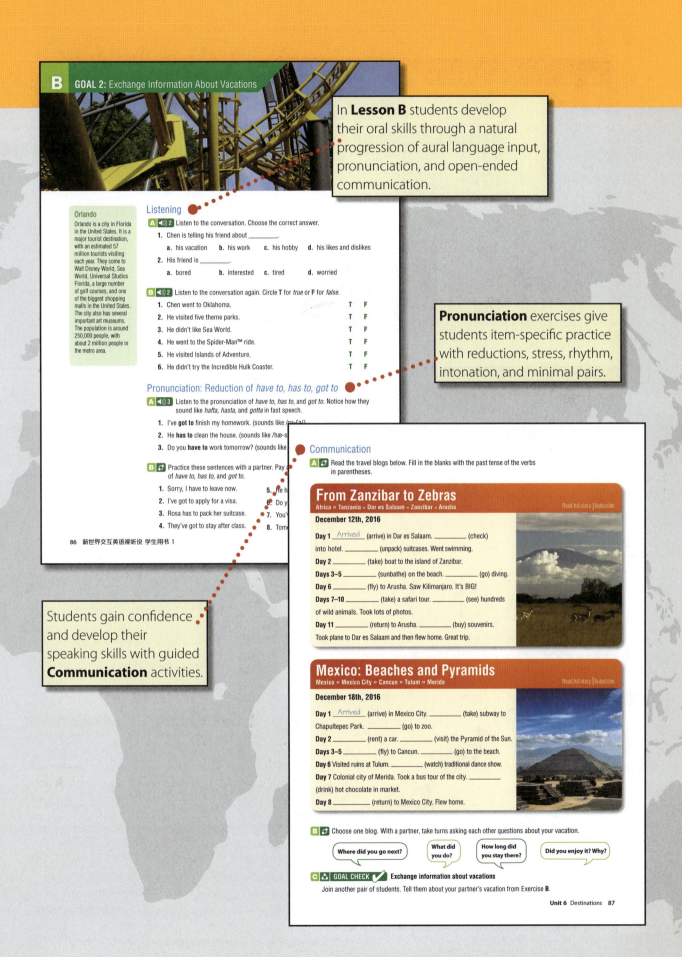

UNIT WALK-THROUGH

C GOAL 3: Describe a Personal Experience

Language Expansion: Emphatic adjectives

A For each picture below, choose two or three emphatic adjectives from the chart and write them down.

Adjectives	Emphatic adjectives			
good/nice	excellent	outstanding	magnificent	amazing
bad	awful	terrible	horrible	
interesting	fascinating			
tiring	exhausting			
dirty	filthy			
clean	spotless			
big	enormous	huge		

> **Language Expansion** sections focus on specific areas that help students build language strategies and become more competent users of English.

D GOAL 4: Share Special Travel Tips with Others

Listening

A Discuss the questions with a partner.
1. What documents should you take when you travel abroad?
2. What should be packed in your bags when traveling abroad?
3. What do you think you should prepare if you are to take a flight at the airport?

B 🔊 5 Listen to the passage. Fill in the blanks.
The traveling expert Mike Connelly wrote a book named _____, in which he shared some pointers on _____, _____, and _____.

C 🔊 5 Listen to the passage again. Circle **T** for *true* or **F** for *false*.
1. Some countries refuse to allow people to enter if their passport expires in less than six months. T F
2. Copies of your important documents and credit card should be kept in another bag. T F
3. Your house keys should be packed in your check-in luggage. T F
4. You'd better use good bags while traveling. T F
5. Airline food is usually good. T F

D 🔊 5 Listen to the passage again and answer the questions.
1. Do you think the author enjoys traveling?
2. Why should you check the expiration date of your passport?
3. Why should you tie a sock to your bag?
4. Why should you take a good book when you travel?

> **Word Focus** boxes provide definitions of additional vocabulary, useful collocations, and special usage.

Word Focus
expiration date the date a thing comes to an end or can no longer be used

Real Language
We use the expression *share some pointers* to say *give advice*.

> **Real Language** information boxes in every unit focus students' attention on frequently used phrases and how to use them.

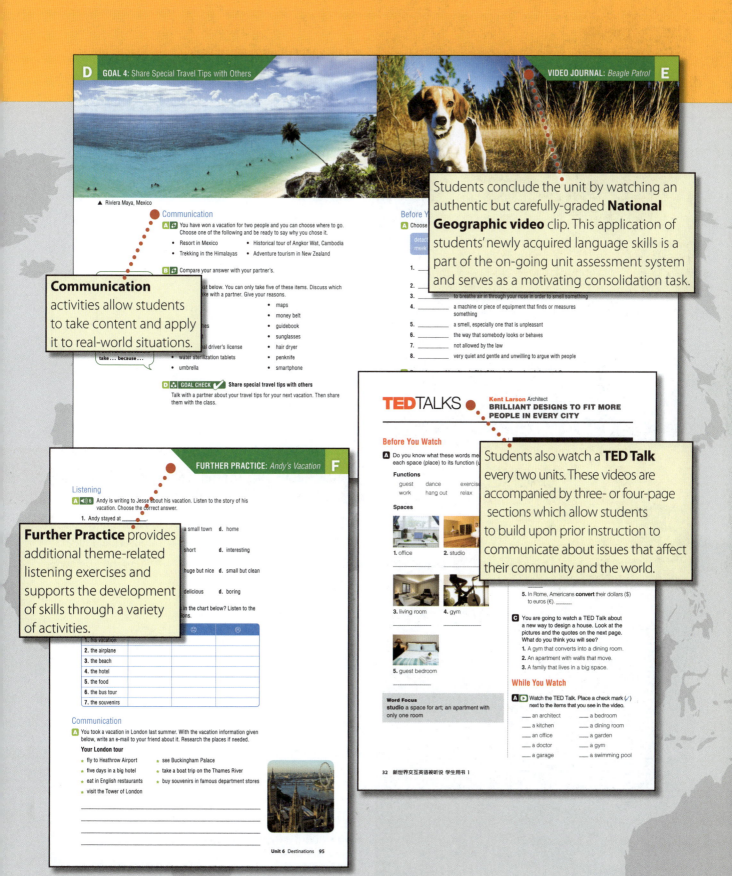

Unit Walk-Through   vii

CONTENTS

	Unit Goals	Vocabulary
UNIT 1 — Transitions — Page 2	• Talk about milestones in your life • Talk about the best age to do something • Use *how* questions to get more information • Describe an important transition in your life	Stages of life Adjectives for age
UNIT 2 — Luxuries — Page 14	• Explain how we get luxury items • Talk about needs and wants • Discuss what makes people's lives better • Evaluate the effect of advertising	Luxury items Import/Export items

TEDTALKS Video Page 27 **Charlie Todd: The Shared Experience of Absurdity**

	Unit Goals	Vocabulary
UNIT 3 — Nature — Page 32 	• Use conditionals to talk about real situations • Talk about possible future situations • Describe what animals do • Discuss a problem in nature	Nouns and adjectives to describe animals Adverbs of manner
UNIT 4 — Life in the Past — Page 46	• Discuss life in the past • Contrast different ways of life • Compare today with the past • Talk about a historical wonder	Life in the past Separable phrasal verbs

TEDTALKS Video Page 59 **Hans Rosling: The Magic Washing Machine**

Listening	Speaking and Pronunciation	Video Journal	Further Practice
General and focused listening A radio program: Healthy tips from an Okinawan centenarian **TEDTALKS** "Living Beyond Limits"	Talking about something you did Discussing the best age for life transitions The schwa sound /ə/ in unstressed syllables	**National Geographic:** "Nubian Wedding"	"Celebrating Transitions"
Focused listening Discussions: The world flower market **National Geographic:** "Perfume: The Essence of Illusion"	Discussing luxuries and necessities Talking about improving your life Sentence stress—content words vs. function words	**National Geographic:** "Coober Pedy Opals"	"Where Does Silk Come From"
General and focused listening A radio program: The bluefin tuna **TEDTALKS** "How Poachers Became Caretakers"	Talk about issues that affect nature Role-playing to promote environmental action to make oceans sustainable Phrases in sentences	**National Geographic:** "Happy Elephants"	"Elephants or People?"
General and focused listening A lecture: The Sami people **National Geographic:** "Lord of the Mongols"	Talking about how technology has changed our lives Discussing daily life in the past Reduction of *used to*	**National Geographic:** "Searching for Genghis Khan"	"Living History at Jamestown Settlement"

CONTENTS

		Unit Goals	Vocabulary
UNIT 5	**Careers** Page 64	• Discuss career choices • Ask and answer job-related questions • Talk about career planning • Talk about innovative jobs	Careers and jobs Participial adjectives
UNIT 6	**Celebrations** Page 78	• Describe a festival • Compare holidays in different countries • Talk about celebrations • Share opinions about holidays	Festivals and holidays Expressions for celebrations

TEDTALKS Video Page 91 **Beverly and Dereck Joubert: Life Lessons from Big Cats**

		Unit Goals	Vocabulary
UNIT 7	**The Mind** Page 96	• Talk about learning strategies • Talk about your senses • Talk about your fears • Describe an emotional experience	Thought processes Scientific studies
UNIT 8	**Changing Planet** Page 108	• Suggest solutions to environmental problems • Discuss causes and effects • Talk about invasive species • Discuss effects on the future	Environmental changes Large numbers

TEDTALKS Video Page 122 **Sylvia Earle: My Wish—Protect Our Oceans**

Listening	Speaking and Pronunciation	Video Journal	Further Practice

General and focused listening
An interview:
   A restaurant owner
   in Thailand
 	
TEDTALKS
"Making Filthy Water Drinkable"
	Discussing career choices Intonation in questions	**National Geographic:**
		"Trinidad Bird Man"
			"Dream Jobs: Mona Davis"

General and focused listening Discussions: Local celebrations or holidays **National Geographic:** "Starting a New Tradition"	Comparing different international celebrations Talking about personal celebrations Question intonation with lists	**National Geographic:** "Young Riders of Mongolia"	"The Oldest Celebration in the World"
Listening for general understanding and specific information A radio program about the unusual condition of synesthesia **National Geographic:** "In Your Face"	Talking about sensations *Th* sounds	**National Geographic:** "Memory Man"	"The Mind-Body Connection"
General and focused listening Climate change **TED**TALKS "Salvation (and Profit) in Greentech"	Discussing cause and effect Linking words together	**National Geographic:** "The Netherlands: Rising Water"	"What Can One City Do?"

UNIT 1
Transitions

Kosavar Bosnian bride preparing for traditional wedding in Donje Ljubinje located in the Shar Mountains between Kosovo and Macedonia

Look at the photo, then answer the questions:

1. What is happening in the picture?
2. What are some important *transitions* in life?

UNIT 1 GOALS

1. Talk about milestones in your life
2. Talk about the best age to do something
3. Use *how* questions to get more information
4. Describe an important transition in your life

A GOAL 1: Talk About Milestones in Your Life

Vocabulary

A Complete the photo captions with a phrase from the box.

> an adult   a baby
> a senior citizen
> a teenager   a child

▲ Adolescence
He's _____.

▲ Adulthood
She's _____.

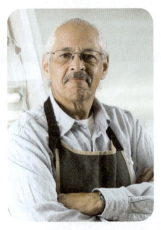
▲ Old Age
He's _____.

▲ Infancy
He's _____.

▲ Childhood
She's _____.

> A baby can't walk or talk.
> A child...

B What do you think? At what age do people make these transitions and what changes take place in these transitions?

Transitions	Ages	Changes
from infancy to childhood		
from childhood to adolescence		
from adolescence to adulthood		
from adulthood to old age		

C Compare your answers in Exercise **B** with your partner's answers to find out how they vary. Give your reasons.

▲ City of Los Angeles, U.S.A

Conversation

A 🔊 1 Listen to the conversation and answer the questions.

1. Where did Jason go?
   _____

2. Did Jason stay at the hotel?
   _____

B 🔊 1 Listen to the conversation again and write it down.

Rick: _____
Jason: _____
Rick: _____
Jason: _____
Rick: _____
Jason: _____

C Practice the conversation with a partner. Then make a new conversation about your travel experiences.

D GOAL CHECK ✓ Talk about milestones in your life

Look at the stages of life on Page 4. Write a question about a milestone (very important event) for each stage. Ask a partner your questions.

> Where were you born?

> How long have you known your best friend?

Unit 1 Transitions 5

B GOAL 2: Talk About the Best Age to Do Something

Listening

A Discuss the questions with a partner.
1. Who is the oldest person you know? How old is he or she?
2. What does this person usually do every day?

B 🔊 2 Listen to a radio program about Ushi Okushima, a woman from Okinawa, Japan. Answer the questions.
1. Where does Ushi work? _____
2. Why is Ushi unusual? _____

C 🔊 2 Listen again and find the information needed below.
1. More than 700 people in Okinawa _____.
2. Three reasons for this:
   a. _____
   b. _____
   c. _____
3. Ushi's advice:
   a. _____
   b. _____
   c. _____

▲ Portrait of a 104-year-old Okinawan woman

D Would you like to live to be 100? Discuss the question with a partner. Give your reasons.

Pronunciation: The schwa sound /ə/ in unstressed syllables

A 🔊 3 Listen to the words. Notice the vowel sound of the unstressed syllables in blue. This is the schwa sound /ə/, and it's the most common vowel sound in English.

infant   lettuce   children   population   adult

B 🔊 4 Listen and repeat the words. Circle the unstressed syllables with the /ə/ sound.

| alone | lesson | person | banana | parents |
| paper | challenge | language | national | chicken |

Conversation

A 🔊 5 Listen to the conversation and answer the questions.

1. How old is Jamal?
   _____

2. When did Jamal have his first part-time job?
   _____

> **Real Language**
>
> You can say *Oh, I don't know about that* to disagree politely with someone.

B 🔊 5 Listen to the conversation again and fill in the blanks.

Andrea: Did you hear the big news? Jamal is getting his own apartment!

Kim: Seriously? But _____ ! That's too young _____.

Andrea: Oh, I don't know about that.

Kim: Do you think he's old enough?

Andrea: Well, _____ , and he's had a part-time job _____.

Kim: That's true... but I think _____.

Andrea: Really? What do you think is the best age to live on your own?

Kim: I think _____.

Andrea: That's a good point. I plan to live with my parents while I'm in college.

C Practice the conversation with a partner. Switch roles and practice it again.

D Make a chart with a partner in your notebooks. Use your own ideas. Then make new conversations about Jorge and Melissa using the conversation in Exercise **B** as an example.

"Jorge is too old to change jobs."	"Melissa is too young to get her own apartment."
Age: _____	Age: _____
Reasons why it is or isn't OK _____	Reasons why it is or isn't OK _____
The best age for this is _____.	The best age for this is _____.

E Read the opinions. How old do you think each person is?

1. "He's too old to play soccer."   Age: _____
2. "He's too young to travel alone."   Age: _____
3. "She's too old to dance."   Age: _____
4. "She's too young to drive a car."   Age: _____
5. "She's too old to learn a new language." Age: _____
6. "He's too old to get married."   Age: _____

F **GOAL CHECK** ✓ **Talk about the best age to do something**

Look at your answers to Exercise **E**. Compare your answers with your partner's, and explain your opinions. What is the best age for each of these things? Do you know someone who does these things at an unusual age?

Unit 1 Transitions   7

C GOAL 3: Use *How* Questions to Get More Information

Language Expansion: Adjectives for age

A Do you know someone who fits any of these descriptions? Who is it? Share your answers with a partner. Use the adjectives in the box to help you.

youthful	older, but with the energy of a young person (good)
childish	older, but acting like a child (bad)
elderly	looking and acting old
mature	old enough to be responsible and make good decisions
middle-aged	not young or old (about 40–60)
in his / her twenties	between 20 and 29 (also in his *teens*, *thirties*, *forties*, etc.)
retired	stopped working full-time (often after 65)

B Talk about these people with a partner. How old are they? Describe them with adjectives from the box in Exercise **A**.

Word Focus

age limit the oldest or youngest age that you can do something

come of age become an adult

I think she's in her teens, but she looks very mature.

How + adjective or adverb

How + adjective or adverb	
Adjectives give information about nouns. Use *How* + adjective to ask a question about a descriptive adjective.	Lenora is very **mature**. **How mature** is she? She's mature enough to babysit my son.
Adverbs give information about verbs. Use *How* + adverb to ask a question about an adverb.	I **learn quickly**. **How quickly** do you learn? I learned to ride a bicycle in one day!

A Unscramble the questions. Take turns with a partner asking the questions.

1. English how do speak well you ___How well do you speak English___?
2. you studying how been English long have _____?
3. can fast you how type _____?
4. back you how will soon be _____?
5. your family how often move does _____?

B Complete the conversations. Write questions using *how*.

1. **A:** I think Mr. Chen is too elderly to live alone.
   B: He doesn't look old to me. _____?
2. **A:** My brother failed his driver's license test six times because he drives so badly.
   B: Wow! _____?
3. **A:** I can't go to the movie with you tonight, because my first class is very early tomorrow.
   B: That's too bad. _____?
4. **A:** I don't want to get my own apartment. It's much too expensive.
   B: Really? _____?
5. **A:** I haven't finished reading the assignment for tomorrow. I guess I read too slowly.
   B: That's a problem. _____?

Elizabeth, in her 60s
- started on a trip around the world
- independent

reasons: _____
_____
_____
_____

Conversation

A 🔊 6 Close your book and listen to the conversation. What did Erik get?

Mrs. Ryan: My son Erik just got his first credit card.
Mrs. Chen: He's still a university student.
Mrs. Ryan: That's true, but he has always been careful with money.
Mrs. Chen: Really? How careful is he?
Mrs. Ryan: He's very careful. In high school he saved enough money to buy a computer.
Mrs. Chen: Then maybe he is ready to get a credit card.

B Practice the conversation with a partner. Switch roles and practice again.

C Complete the descriptions on the right. Then make new conversations.

D **GOAL CHECK** ✓ **Use *how* questions to get more information**

Take turns with a partner giving a description of yourself or how you do something. Ask questions with *how* to get as much information as possible.

Keisha, 19
- got her own apartment
- mature

reasons: _____
_____
_____
_____
_____

Unit 1 Transitions 9

D   GOAL 4: Describe an Important Transition in Your Life

" ... It's not about breaking down borders; it's about pushing off of them and seeing what amazing places they might bring us. "

—Amy Purdy

Amy Purdy's idea worth spreading is that obstacles don't have to stop us—they can help us to get creative. Watch Purdy's full TED Talk on TED.com.

Word Focus

amputee a person who has had an arm or a leg removed by surgery
patchwork pieces of cloth that are sewn in a pattern
prosthetic an artificial device that replaces a missing part of the body
let go of to stop thinking or worrying about something
embrace to accept readily or gladly
take charge of to take control of
non-profit not done for money
inspiration a sudden feeling of enthusiasm or a new idea that helps you to create something

Listening

A Check (✓) the items below that show a transition in life. Share your ideas with a partner.

_____ 1. get a new job
_____ 2. go shopping
_____ 3. buy a car
_____ 4. begin college or university
_____ 5. play soccer
_____ 6. get married

B 🔊 7 Listen to the passage. Circle the correct option.

1. Amy Purdy is a champion (cyclist | snowboarder).
2. She has prosthetic (arms | legs).
3. Purdy (imagined | remembered) her new life.
4. Purdy's (book | organization) is called "Adaptive Action Sports."

C 🔊 7 Listen to the passage again. Write **T** for *true* or **F** for *false* next to the statements.

_____ 1. Amy Purdy nearly died when she was 19.
_____ 2. It wasn't difficult for her to recover from her illness.
_____ 3. During her recovery, Purdy decided to control her life again.
_____ 4. She helps other people by sharing her story with them.
_____ 5. Purdy worked as a model before her illness.

D How do you think you would react in Purdy's situation? Share your ideas.

▲ After becoming disabled, Amy Purdy imagined—and now lives—a very full life.

Communication

A Circle the correct phrasal verbs in the sentences.

1. You have to (believe in | yield to) yourself. That's the secret of success.
2. The man who has (made up | made out) his mind to win will never say "impossible".
3. If you want to make a change in your life, you need to (take charge of | get over) it.
4. Transitions can be difficult, but if you (keep on | grow up) trying, you'll succeed.
5. Learning to snowboard was so challenging that Purdy nearly (set out | gave up).
6. At the start of term, he vowed to (turn over | turn in) a new leaf and study harder.

B Think about an important transition that you made in your life. What caused it? What effects did it have? Share your ideas with a partner.

C **GOAL CHECK** ✓ **Describe an important transition in your life**

Share your ideas about transitions. What are some positive/negative reasons for making transitions?

Unit 1 Transitions 11

E VIDEO JOURNAL: *Nubian Wedding*

Nubian women sing traditional songs as they arrive with gifts at the home of a newly-wedded bride.

Before You Watch

A Talk with a partner about weddings that each of you has seen. Use the topics and the question in the box to help you.

> the bride   the groom
> the party   the ceremony
> How were the two weddings similar or different?

While You Watch

A Watch the video. Number the parts of the wedding in order.

_____ Everyone eats a special dinner.

___1___ The bride and groom sign special legal papers.

_____ The groom puts a ring on the bride's finger.

_____ The bride's skin is painted.

_____ The groom leaves his parents' house.

B Watch the video again. Answer the questions.

1. When did Sheriff meet Abir? _____
2. How many days does the wedding last? _____
3. When does the party start each day? _____
4. When did life change for the Nubians? _____
5. What do people eat at the wedding? _____
6. Who kisses the groom? _____

After You Watch/Communication

A What surprised you the most about the Nubian wedding? How is it similar to or different from weddings in China?

Further Practice: *Celebrating Transitions* **F**

Listening

A 🔊 8 Listen to the passage and complete the following chart.

	Transitions		
	Schulanfang	*Quince Años*	*Coming-of-Age Day*
Country			
Age of people celebrating			
When			
Where			
What do people do?			

B Answer the questions.

1. Which of these celebrations sounds like the most fun? Why?
   _____
   _____

2. Which birthdays are the most important in your family? Why?
   _____
   _____

C Talk about a celebration of a life transition such as a birthday party or commencement. Who was it for? What were you celebrating? What did you do? Why was it important?

Unit 1 Transitions 13

UNIT 2 Luxuries

Baroque dinning room for Carnival party in Venice, Italy

Look at the photo, then answer the questions:

1. What is a luxury?
2. What are the most desirable luxuries?

UNIT 2 GOALS

1. Explain how we get luxury items
2. Talk about needs and wants
3. Discuss what makes people's lives better
4. Evaluate the effect of advertising

A GOAL 1: Explain How We Get Luxury Items

Vocabulary

pearl necklace
silver
diamonds
fur coat
emeralds
silk shirt
gold
expensive watch

▲ luxury clothing
_____
_____

▲ precious stones
_____
_____

▲ handmade jewelry
_____
_____

▲ precious metals
_____
_____

A Write each word or phrase from the box in the correct category above.

B Write three things China imports and three things China exports in your notebook. Share your lists with the class.

China imports (buys from other countries)	China exports (sells to other countries)

C Take turns. Tell a partner about a luxury item you have or want to have. What is it? Why do you like it? Where can someone get it? How is it made?

Conversation

A 🔊 1 Listen to the conversation and choose the correct answer.

1. a. women in Egypt
   b. women in India
   c. women in Sri Lanka
   d. not mentioned

2. a. The blouse is cotton.
   b. The best cotton is grown in Egypt.
   c. A lot of cotton is grown in India.
   d. Women work together in a co-op.

> **Word Focus**
>
> **mined** removed from under the Earth's surface
> **co-op** a cooperative society where members share benefits and advantages

B 🔊 1 Listen to the conversation again and fill in the blanks.

Sandra: _____?

Ellen: No, it's cotton, but it is soft like silk.

Sandra: _____.

Ellen: Really? _____, too, but I don't know which kind is better.

Sandra: Where was your blouse made?

Ellen: In Sri Lanka. _____.
They work together to make clothes. Then _____
_____.

Sandra: That's great!

C 🔄 Practice the conversation with a partner. Switch roles and practice it again.

D 🔄 **GOAL CHECK** ✓ **Explain how we get luxury items**

What luxury items are popular in China? If the items are imported, where are they made? What are they made from? Who makes them? Tell a partner.

Unit 2 Luxuries 17

B GOAL 2: Talk About Needs and Wants

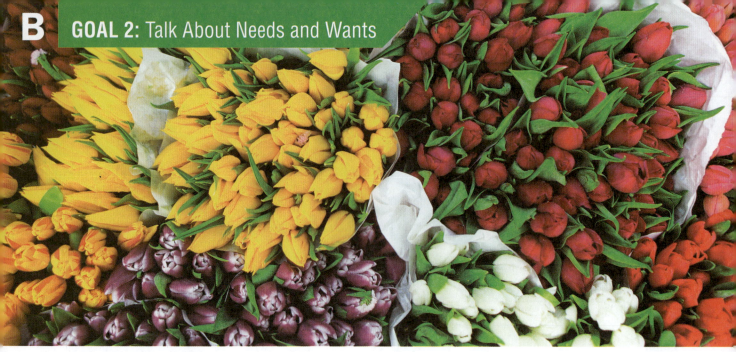

▲ Bouquets of roses for sale at a flower market

▲ a greenhouse

Listening

A 🔊 2 Listen to three people talk about the cut-flower industry. Why is each country important to the flower industry?

1. Japan _____
2. Ecuador _____
3. The Netherlands _____

a. has a good climate for growing flowers.
b. imports many flowers.
c. develops new kinds of flowers.

B 🔊 2 Listen again. Why is the flower industry important to each person?

1. Shinobu: _____
2. Rafael: _____
3. Peter: _____

Pronunciation: Content vs. function words

In sentences, content words have specific meaning and receive greater stress. Other words have a grammatical function and receive less stress.

Content words				
nouns	main verbs	question words	adjectives	adverbs
money	speak	why, where, how	wonderful	easily

More function words	Function words				
conjunctions	pronouns	auxiliary verbs	the verb *be*	articles	prepositions
and, or, but, so	it, she, him	have, is, will, could	is, are, was	the, a(n)	in, to, of, at

18 新世界交互英语视听说 学生用书 3

A 🔊 3 Listen to the stress in each sentence. Then listen again and repeat.

1. She <u>wants</u> to <u>go</u> to a <u>private</u> <u>college</u>.
2. We <u>have</u> to <u>pay</u> the <u>electric</u> <u>bill</u>.
3. The <u>bill</u> can be <u>paid</u> <u>online</u>.
4. My <u>family</u> <u>needs</u> the <u>money</u> I <u>make</u>.
5. I'm <u>saving</u> <u>money</u> for a <u>new</u> <u>computer</u>.
6. He <u>wants</u> a <u>Lexus</u>, but he should <u>buy</u> a <u>Toyota</u>.

B Underline the content words. Then practice saying the sentences with a partner.

1. Flowers are an important part of life.
2. Delicious grapes can be grown in California.
3. I like diamonds and rubies, but they're very expensive.
4. My future could be very bright.
5. Celia wants to buy a new car.
6. Do you think she should get a small car?

> **For Your Information**
> **The cut-flower industry**
> Many cut flowers that are sold for holidays come from great distances. For example, in England, a quarter of the flowers sold on Valentine's Day are grown in Kenya, and many of the others come from Tanzania, Ethiopia, or Uganda. In North America, a large percentage of cut flowers are grown in Colombia. Many people are concerned about the growth of this industry, because workers are exposed to large quantities of toxic chemicals every day. They also object to growing luxury flowers on farmland that could grow food for hungry people.

Communication

A Write each item in the appropriate column. Use your own opinion.

| a computer | a car | furniture | shoes | clean water | fresh fruit |
| books | flowers | money | a telephone | public parks | the Internet |

Luxuries	Necessities

> **Word Focus**
>
> **Necessities** are things we need, such as food and shelter.
>
> **Luxuries** are things we don't really need, but they can be nice to have.

B Compare your chart from Exercise **A** with a partner's chart. Talk about why you think people need (or don't need) the items.

C "Little luxuries" are things that don't cost a lot of money but you enjoy very much, such as *a cup of gourmet coffee*, *a bar of fancy bath soap*, etc. Talk about your little luxuries.

D GOAL CHECK ✓ **Talk about needs and wants**

What is something you absolutely need? What luxury item do you want very much? Discuss these questions with a partner.

C GOAL 3: Discuss What Makes People's Lives Better

Persian rugs are still made by hand in parts of Iran.

Language Expansion

lose–lost
find–found
send–sent
give–given
put–put
freeze–frozen
build–built
know–known

A Fill in the blanks with the words in the box. Use your dictionary to help you.

1. Many kinds of precious stones can be _____ in Brazil.
2. Fresh seafood can be _____ by plane to anywhere in the world.
3. The seafood is _____ so that it stays cold until it arrives.
4. Iran is _____ for its beautiful handmade rugs.
5. Smartphones are _____ every day when they fall out of a pocket or purse.
6. Gifts are often _____ to people on their birthday.
7. Ferrari cars are _____ by hand, so it takes longer to make them.
8. The watches are _____ into special boxes to protect them.

Passive voice with *by*

The passive voice is usually used without a *by* phrase.	Cut flowers **are sold** early in the morning. Most of these cut flowers **are imported**.
A *by* phrase is used when we want to say who or what does something (*the agent*).	These blouses **are made** by well-paid workers. Each rug **is made** by a different artist, so no two rugs are alike.

A Read the sentences and cross out the unimportant *by* phrases.

1. The Mercedes-Benz is made in Germany ~~by people~~.
2. This necklace was given to me by my grandmother.
3. King Tut's tomb was discovered by Howard Carter.
4. My car was stolen on April 19 by someone.
5. The company was founded by the owner's grandfather.
6. Even during the winter, daisies can be grown in greenhouses by workers.

Conversation

A 🔊 4 Listen to the conversation and answer the questions.

1. According to Gary, why is education valuable?
   _____

2. How does education improve Gary's life?
   _____

B 🔊 4 Listen to the conversation again and fill in the blanks.

Lance: Gary, do you think people's lives _____?

Gary: _____. Some people don't have enough money _____. Their lives are _____.

Lance: What about other people?

Gary: Well, when you have enough money _____, I think your life can be _____.

Lance: Interesting! _____?

Gary: Sure. _____, and I hope to get a good job someday _____.

Lance: I see what you mean. For me, though, my life would be improved by _____.

Gary: OK, but nice cars cost money. Maybe you should _____.

Real Language

We use *It depends* to say that something is not always true. Then we often explain our reasons.

▲ College campus in the spring

C 🔁 Practice the conversation with a partner. Switch roles and practice it again.

D 🔁 **GOAL CHECK** ✓ **Discuss what makes people's lives better**

Which of these things improves people's lives the most? Rank them in order of importance from 1 (most) to 4 (least). Then explain your answers.

1. _____ improves people's lives the most because _____

2. _____ improves people's lives the least because _____

money ____   a nice house ____   good health ____   a good job ____

Unit 2 Luxuries 21

D GOAL 4: Evaluate the Effect of Advertising

Listening

A 🔄 Discuss these questions with a partner.

1. Have you ever bought perfume? What brand did you buy?
2. Why do people wear perfume?
3. What do ads for perfume usually show?

B 🔊 5 Listen to the first part of the passage and fill in the table.

Main ingredients in perfume	
Types of flowers used to make perfumes	
The city famous for flower farms	
Sources of ingredients	

C 🔊 6 Listen to the second part of the passage and fill in the blanks.

The _____ of natural ingredients is just one of the reasons that perfumers today also use _____ ingredients in their fragrances. In addition, synthetics allow perfumers to use scents that cannot be gotten naturally; for example, the scent from the lilac flower. They allow the use of scents from rare or _____ flowers, and they save wild animals from being used for their musk—a kind of fixative. According to perfumer Harry Fremont, "Good fragrance is a balance between _____."

Once perfumers have created a lovely fragrance, it's time for the marketing department to _____. The industry spends hundreds of millions of dollars each year to convince people to buy something they don't really need. The success rate for new perfumes is low—only about _____ is successful, so spending money on _____ is a big risk. It's also the only way to let the world know about a fragrance so _____ that it can make us believe our dreams will come true.

D 👥 Make a list of other products designed to make people feel better about themselves. Share your list with the class and talk about whether the products really do what they're supposed to do.

For Your Information Perfume

The word perfume comes from the Latin "per fumum" meaning through smoke. The first perfumes were made in ancient Mesopotamia (Iraq) and Egypt. Knowledge of how to make perfume was brought to Europe by the Muslims, and the first European perfume was made in Hungary. In Europe, the original purpose of perfume was to cover the odors of unwashed bodies. By the 18th century, Grasse and Paris had become the world centers for perfume. Today, the job of inventing new perfumes is done by a person called a nez—the French word for "nose".

Flower plantation in Grasse, France

D | GOAL 4: Evaluate the Effect of Advertising

Listening

A 🔊 7 Listen to the passage. Circle **T** for *true* or **F** for *false*.

1. In the digital age, few newspapers and magazines are printed on paper.   T   F
2. Print ads enable companies to choose their audience.   T   F
3. One of the advantages of the print ads is that the audience can spend as much time as they would like to look at it.   T   F
4. Print ads must have three things in common: a photograph, a message and a design.   T   F
5. A successful print ad needs to appeal to everyone.   T   F

B You are in charge of marketing a new perfume. Discuss the questions.

1. Who is your target audience? (men or women, young or old, etc.)
2. What kind of photograph might appeal to that audience?
3. What is your message? (What do you want the audience to think or do?)
4. What are some key words to include in your message?

C Write a print ad for your perfume.

D | **GOAL CHECK** ✓ **Evaluate the effect of advertising**

Choose a luxury item and talk with a partner about the way it is marketed. What forms of advertising are used? How do the advertisers "convince people to buy something they don't really need"?

VIDEO JOURNAL: *Coober Pedy Opals* E

Opals mined in Australia

Southern Australia, Australia

Before You Watch

A Match each word in blue with its definition in the box.

1. The ground under Coober Pedy contains opals. _____
2. Digging is one thing you can do in the ground. _____
3. The Australian outback is very dry and hot. _____
4. Very beautiful opals can be worth a fortune. _____
5. Miners hope for a big payoff for their hard work. _____

a. area that is far away from cities
b. a large sum of money
c. earth, soil
d. the benefit you get from an action
e. to make a hole by taking away earth

digging   fortune
outback   payoff   ground

While You Watch

A ▶ Watch the video. Circle each word in the box when you hear it.

B ▶ Watch the video again. Circle **T** for *true* or **F** for *false*.

1. About three thousand people live in Coober Pedy.   T   F
2. Over eighty percent of all opals come from Australia.   T   F
3. Ninety-five percent of all opals are colorless.   T   F
4. The hope of a huge payoff motivates people to dig for opals. T   F
5. Most people in Coober Pedy make a fortune eventually.   T   F

Word Focus

miners people who dig for stones or other minerals

After You Watch/Communication

A Some of the tunnels in Coober Pedy are converted into homes. What might be the advantages and disadvantages of these underground homes? Tell a partner.

B Create a newspaper or Internet job listing for opal miners. Describe the work and the potential rewards. Try to attract new people to Coober Pedy!

F Further Practice: *Where Does Silk Come From*

Listening

A 🔊 8 Listen to the passage and number the following pictures to show the steps for making silk.

  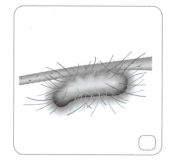 

B 🔊 8 Listen to the passage again and answer the questions.

1. Why do people like to wear silk?
2. Do you use or wear anything made of silk? Why or why not?

C Imagine you have won a contest and you can choose your prize. Which of these luxuries do you want for your prize? Why?

> a gold watch   1 kilogram of caviar   a diamond ring
> 1,000 red roses   a painting by a famous artist   1 liter of perfume

Charlie Todd Comedian, Founder of Improv Everywhere
THE SHARED EXPERIENCE OF ABSURDITY

Before You Watch

> Charlie Todd's idea worth spreading is that play is a good thing—however old you are. Watch Todd's full TED Talk on TED.com.

A Look at the picture and answer the questions with a partner.

1. Where are these people?
2. What do people usually do here?
3. What are these people doing?

B Charlie Todd is a man who delights in creating unexpected scenes like the one in the picture above. Here are some words you will hear in his TED Talk. Complete the paragraph with the correct form of the word. Not all words will be used.

> **cop** *n.* a police officer
> **diverse** *adj.* made up of people or things that are different from each other
> **improvise** *v.* to speak or perform without preparation
> **inspire** *v.* to give (someone) an idea about what to do or create
> **play** *n.* activities that are done especially by children for fun or enjoyment
> **prank** *n.* a trick that is done to someone usually as a joke

Improv Everywhere is a group that creates _____ in public places. Their founder, Charlie Todd, believes that _____ is as important for adults as it is for kids. He was _____ to start the group when he couldn't find a regular theater to perform in. Now, Improv Everywhere's _____ members can be found all around the world. So the next time a group of people are _____ on the street or a store, you might be seeing an Improv Everywhere performance.

C Look at the pictures on the next page. Check (✓) the information that you predict you will hear in the TED Talk.

___ 1. We perform in many different public places.
___ 2. Our goal is to make people smile and laugh.
___ 3. Our performances are only for paying audiences.

Charlie Todd Comedian, Founder of Improv Everywhere
THE SHARED EXPERIENCE OF ABSURDITY

While You Watch

A ▶ Watch the TED Talk. Circle the main idea.

1. Charlie Todd couldn't find work as an actor.
2. Everyone needs to be creative and have fun.
3. Improv Everywhere creates pranks that are positive experiences.

B ▶ Look at the photos. Watch the TED Talk again and write the letter of the caption under the correct photo.

a. Improv Everywhere's pranks take place in public places.
b. Nobody expects to see characters from a movie at the library.
c. Getting a high five on your way to work might make your day better.
d. Charlie Todd wants to share a sense of fun and play.

1. ___

2. ___

3. ___

4. _a_

Challenge! Some people might object to Improv Everywhere's pranks. Why? Are Improv Everywhere's pranks a good idea or a bad idea? Tell a partner. Give examples to support your idea.

> "There is no point and (...) there doesn't have to be a point. We don't need a reason. As long as it's fun."
> —Charlie Todd

Charlie Todd Comedian, Founder of Improv Everywhere
THE SHARED EXPERIENCE OF ABSURDITY

After You Watch

A Complete the summary with the words in the box.

Charlie Todd _____ that we should be having more fun. In 2005, he staged an Improv Everywhere prank when he asked a group of friends to _____ in the window frames of a building. Todd calls their _____ "missions", and the _____ are "secret agents." Since the first prank, Todd and his group have _____ more than 100 missions and some of them have become an international _____.

> stand   actors
> believes   completed
> event   performances

B Match the phrases to the information from the TED Talk.

_____ 1. number of high fives Rob gave   **a.** 2006
_____ 2. number of agents participating in "Blue Shirt" mission   **b.** 8
_____ 3. number of windows in the building   **c.** 80
_____ 4. year he was inspired to do "Blue Shirt" mission   **d.** 2,000
_____ 5. age of one young "secret agent"   **e.** 70

C Circle the statements that paraphrase Charlie Todd's ideas.
1. When I moved to New York, I wanted to be famous.
2. I started performing in public because I couldn't use a theater.
3. We want to create performances that make people happy.
4. Riding the subway in New York is a pleasant experience.
5. Adults need to learn to play again.

Project

Charlie Todd and his group Improv Everywhere are on a mission to make New Yorkers laugh. They play pranks in public places, creating shared, positive experiences. Use Todd's ideas to design an improvised performance in your own city.

A Look at the list of places Improv Everywhere "agents" have performed. Circle the ones you think would be the most fun.

| beach | park | public library | store | subway | car | train station |

B Compare your choices in Exercise **A** with your partner's. Where else could you perform in your town or city? Remember that your goal is to create a positive, shared experience for the people who see your performance.

C Work with a group. Decide where you will perform and what activity you will do. Give each person in your group something specific to do. Use the table to organize your ideas.

Place	Date & Time	Activity	People

Challenge! Charlie Todd and Improv Everywhere really are everywhere—they even pulled a prank at TED. Go to TED.com and find out more about the prank they played. How did they do it?

UNIT 3
Nature

Tadpoles swimming around lily stalks

Look at the photo, then answer the questions:

1. What animals are these? Where do they usually live?
2. How do they get their food?

UNIT 3 GOALS

1. Use conditionals to talk about real situations
2. Talk about possible future situations
3. Describe what animals do
4. Discuss a problem in nature

A GOAL 1: Use Conditionals to Talk About Real Situations

POLAR BEAR (*Ursus maritimus*) The polar bear is one of eight different ___ species of bears. Its ___ habitat is the ice and water near the Arctic Circle. These bears are ___ predators that eat other animals. Their usual ___ prey is other arctic animals, such as seals. They ___ hunt for their food during the day. This bear is wild and is found in the north of Canada. Polar bears are ___ vulnerable, and there are not many of them left. Their habitat is ___ shrinking. If we don't protect these bears, they will become ___ extinct.

Vocabulary

A Read the text to the left.

B Match the words in blue to their meanings.

1. to look for animals and kill them
2. an animal that other animals kill to eat
3. animals that kill other animals
4. the place where an animal usually lives
5. a kind of animal or plant
6. no longer in existence, all dead
7. easily damaged or hurt
8. becoming smaller

Real conditionals in the future

A Study the sentence and answer the questions.

Condition   Result
If we don't protect these bears, they will become extinct.

1. Is the condition possible or not possible? _____
2. Is the result now or in the future? _____

Real conditionals in the future	
We use the real conditional for situations that can happen in the future.	**If you look** out the train window, **you will see** a group of wild deer.
Conditional sentences have two clauses: the condition clause and the result clause.	Condition: *if* + subject + simple present tense verb Result: subject + *will/be going to* + verb
The condition clause can be at the beginning or end of the sentence.	**If you talk** loudly, the birds will fly away. The birds are going to fly away **if you talk** loudly.

B Complete the sentence with the correct form of the verb in parentheses.

1. If an elephant _____ (live) in a zoo, it _____ (get) bored.
2. We _____ (be) very happy if our team _____ (win).
3. If I _____ (see) a bear in the forest, I _____ (yell) loudly.
4. I _____ (go) to the concert if I _____ (have) enough money for a ticket.
5. If you _____ (sleep, not) enough, you _____ (feel) tired.

C Discuss the situations with a partner. Write sentences to describe them in your notebook. What will happen if...

1. polar bears can't find enough food?
2. the polar bear's habitat disappears?
3. people put more polar bears in zoos?
4. people protect polar bears?
5. polar bears become extinct?

▲ An Alaskan brown bear near Nonvianuk Lake, Katmai National Park, Alaska

Conversation

A 🔊 1 Close your book and listen to the conversation. What is Katie afraid of?

B 🔊 1 Listen to the conversation again and fill in the blanks. Check your answers with your partner.

Mike: Let's _____.

Katie: I'm not sure that's a good idea. _____.

Mike: That may be, but there aren't very many, _____.

Katie: If I see a bear, _____. They're so dangerous!

Mike: Bears won't hurt you _____.

> **Real Language**
>
> You can say *That may be (true), but...* to show that you disagree with the other person's idea.

C Practice the conversation with a partner. Switch roles and practice it again.

D Make two new conversations. Choose from the topics below.

1. White Beach/sharks
2. North Campground/wolves
3. the nature reserve/snakes
4. your own idea _____

E **GOAL CHECK** ✓ **Use conditionals to talk about real situations**

Look at the problems in the box. How will these issues affect nature? Talk about them with a partner.

> climate change
> human population growth
> energy use

B GOAL 2: Talk About Possible Future Situations

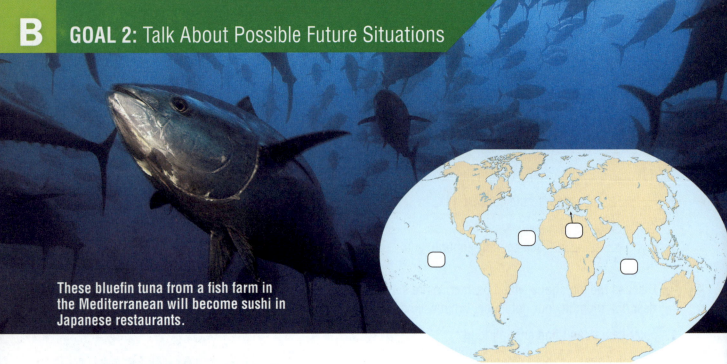

These bluefin tuna from a fish farm in the Mediterranean will become sushi in Japanese restaurants.

1. Atlantic Ocean
2. Pacific Ocean
3. Indian Ocean
4. Mediterranean Sea

Listening

A Look at the map and match the places with the boxes on the map.

B 🔊 2 Listen to the radio program about the bluefin tuna and circle the three places it talks about on the map.

C 🔊 3 Listen and fill in the blanks.

Bluefin Tuna

1. up to _____ feet long
2. weighs more than _____
3. colors: _____ , _____ , _____
4. swims more than _____ miles an hour
5. lives up to _____ years

D 🔊 4 Listen again to the second part of the program and choose the best answer to each question you hear.

1. What can we learn about the bluefin tuna?
   a. It has a lot of fat in its body, which is unsuitable for people to eat.
   b. In Japan, people mainly use it to make sushi and tuna steaks.
   c. They are in danger of disappearing due to overfishing and illegal fishing.
   d. They are quite abundant in the Pacific and Indian Ocean.

2. Which of the following statements is true?
   a. Scientists suggest stopping catching bluefin tuna for several years.
   b. Overfishing has become a big problem because there are no international rules to stop it.
   c. To protect the bluefin tuna from extinction, people should stop eating sushi.
   d. Big boats should be banned from fishing in the Mediterranean.

E Discuss the questions with a partner.

1. Is fish cheap or expensive where you live? How often do you eat it?
2. Do you know where the fish you eat comes from?

Pronunciation: Phrases in sentences

A 🔊 5 Listen and repeat the sentences. Notice how they're divided into phrases.

1. A bluefin tuna | can swim very fast | and live a long time.
2. My friend's birthday | is June fourteenth.

B Draw lines to divide these sentences into phrases.

1. Jeff and I saw three big sharks.
2. Cathy isn't here, but I can take a message.
3. I'll bring my camera if we go to the zoo.
4. If they catch all the big fish, the species won't survive.
5. The family will have fun at the national park.

C 🔊 6 Listen and check your answers. Practice saying the sentences.

Communication

A Read the information. What does *sustainable* mean?

Fish is one of the world's favorite foods. Around the world, the average person eats 36 pounds (16 kg) of fish every year. But many kinds of fish around the world are disappearing because people catch too many of them. Scientists say that 90 percent of the biggest fish are gone now. If we catch too many big fish now, there won't be any baby fish in the future. Our way of fishing now is not **sustainable**— it can't continue for a long time without hurting the environment.

B You are members of an environmental group called **Save the Oceans**. You want to take action to solve the fishing problem. Talk about these plans. What will happen if we follow each one?

> **Word Focus**
>
> The word **environment** can refer to nature or to everything that's around us.
>
> *Recycling used paper is good for the* **environment.**
>
> *This classroom is a good* **environment** *for learning.*

Plan A: Don't eat fish!
Tell people to stop buying and eating fish. Put ads in newspapers and magazines, and make TV commercials to explain why fishing hurts the environment.

Plan B: Safe fish symbol
Make a special symbol for fish that are caught in a sustainable way. Make commercials to tell people to look for this symbol in supermarkets and restaurants.

Plan C: Strict laws about fishing Make stronger laws about how many fish people can catch. Send special police in fast boats to all of the fishing areas to make sure that fishing boats follow the laws.

C **GOAL CHECK** ✓ **Talk about possible future situations**

Which is the best plan? Why? Explain your decision to the class.

C GOAL 3: Describe What Animals Do

Language Expansion: Adverbs of manner

A How do they do it? Complete the sentences with an adverb from the box.

beautifully fast well
slowly loudly badly

1. A snail moves __slowly__.
2. A fox hunts _____.
3. A penguin walks _____.
4. A monkey jumps _____.
5. A lion roars _____.
6. A bird sings _____.

Adverbs of manner	
Adverbs of manner tell us how an action is done. The adverb usually follows the verb.	A snail <u>moves</u> **slowly**. Tigers <u>run</u> **fast**.
Many adverbs of manner are formed from adjectives plus -ly.	quick–quickly safe–safely soft–softly careful–carefully
Some adverbs of manner are irregular.	well fast hard
Note: For most adjectives that end in -y, change the -y to -i and add -ly.	easy–easily happy–happily angry–angrily

quick careful
quiet easy loud

B In your notebook, write sentences using the adverb form of each adjective in the box.

Quantifiers

A 🔊 7 In English, objects are viewed as separate things that we can count or as a whole that we can't count. Listen to a short passage and fill in the missing words, trying to identify count and non-count nouns.

Raccoons are small _____ that live in North America, Japan, and _____. They are omnivores—animals that eat _____.
A raccoon's usual diet is _____. They also like to eat _____.
Sometimes they catch _____.

Quantifiers					
With count nouns			**With non-count nouns**		
too few a few some	a lot of many too many	eggs	too little a little some	a lot of too much	meat

*Quantifiers tell us *how much* or *how many*.
*Don't use *much* in affirmative sentences: ~~He has much money~~. He has a lot of money.

B Circle the correct quantifier in each sentence below.

1. Raccoons eat (many | a little) different kinds of food.
2. They eat (a little | a lot of) nuts.
3. Raccoons will eat (a few | a little) insects if they find them.
4. They sometimes eat (a little | many) soap.
5. If a raccoon goes in your garbage can, you'll find (a lot of | many) garbage all over the place!

Conversation

A 🔊 8 Listen to the conversation and fill in the blanks.

Dan: So, which animals do you want to see at the zoo?

Carmen: I love to look at _____. I think _____.

Dan: Why is that?

Carmen: Well, they _____, but in the water _____ _____. And it's fun to watch them at feeding time.

Dan: Really? What do they eat?

Carmen: _____.

B 👥 Practice the conversation with a partner. Switch roles and practice it again.

C 👥 Fill in the chart. Add your own ideas. Then make new conversations with a partner.

	What they do	What they eat
1. tigers		
2. elephants		

meat walk play
leaves grass swim
run fruit

D 👥 **GOAL CHECK** ✓ **Describe what animals do**

Report to the class. Tell them about your favorite zoo animal. Try to use adverbs and quantifiers.

D GOAL 4: Discuss a Problem in Nature

Many elephants are killed for their tusks.

Listening

A What are some reasons animals are endangered? Talk about your ideas with a partner.

B Look at the list of ways we can protect endangered animals. Check (✓) the ideas you predict you will hear in the passage. Compare your answers with your partner's.

1. _____ stop poaching
2. _____ create advertisements about conservation
3. _____ prevent droughts
4. _____ put land under conservation
5. _____ support nature tourism

C 🔊 9 Listen to the first part of the passage. Write the dates next to the events.

1. _____ 20 lions remain in Kunene
2. _____ John Kasaona is born
3. _____ drought hits Namibia
4. _____ war begins
5. _____ war ends

D 🔊 10 Listen to the second part of the passage and choose the best answer.

1. What can we learn about the Integrated Rural Development and Nature Conservation (IRDNC)?

   a. It's a non-governmental organization made up of local village leaders to protect wildlife.

John Kasaona's idea worth spreading is that there is good news from Africa. Protecting wildlife is a great way to transform communities—and countries. Watch Kasaona's full TED Talk on TED.com.

" We knew conservation would fail if it didn't work to improve the lives of the local communities. "

—John Kasaona

   b. It's a non-governmental organization working in Namibia to protect wildlife.

   c. It's an official organization established by the Namibian government to protect wild animals.

   d. It's a non-governmental organization working in Namibia to educate local poachers.

2. What did IRDNC do to protect the wildlife in Namibia?

   a. It hired a group of local poachers who knew the bush well and understood how wild animals lived.

   b. It hired and worked with a group of village leaders who knew how to deal with local poachers.

   c. It hired a group of wildlife conservation experts who knew the bush and understood how wild animals lived.

   d. It hired Kasaona's father as its leader to help protect wildlife in Namibia.

3. Which of the following is NOT a result of the IRDNC's efforts to protect wildlife in Namibia?

   a. Wild animals are coming back and growing in number.

   b. More land than ever has been put under conservation.

   c. Tourists are coming to the area, which generates money for Namibia to use in education, health care and other important programs.

   d. Namibia has created a model for other nations to follow by severely punishing poachers.

D GOAL 4: Discuss a Problem in Nature

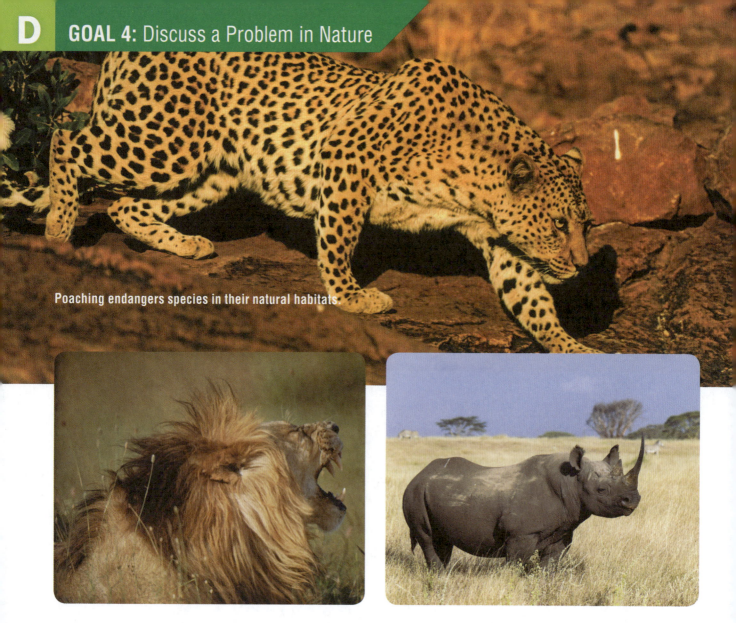

Poaching endangers species in their natural habitats.

Communication

A Think about two or three problems in nature in China. What is happening? What are the causes? Share your ideas with a partner.

B Write *but, so,* and *even though* in the correct places in the paragraph.

By the 1990s, many species of animals were endangered in Namibia. The situation was serious, _____ conservationists needed to find a way to protect the animals. They found one, _____ it wasn't what you would expect: they asked poachers for help. _____ this seemed crazy, I think it was a great idea. If we want to protect endangered species, we need to consider every solution.

> **Speaking Strategy**
> Conjunctions
> Conjunctions are used to connect ideas within sentences.

C GOAL CHECK ✓ Discuss a problem in nature

Work with a group. Share your ideas from Exercise **A** about problems in nature. In your opinion, what is the most important problem to solve? What are two or three ways to help?

VIDEO JOURNAL: *Happy Elephants* — E

Before You Watch

A Read about the video and check the meanings of the words in **bold** with a partner.

> Elephants are amazing animals. They can use their **trunks** to pick up heavy things. **In the wild,** they live in **herds** in the forest. Today, many elephants live in zoos. Their **trainers** take care of them. But can elephants be happy **in captivity**?

While You Watch

A Watch the video. Choose the main idea.

1. Elephants are happier in the wild.
2. People and elephants have been together for a long time.
3. Elephant trainers find ways to make elephants happier.

B Watch the video again. Fill in the blanks.

1. Elephants and people have worked together for over _____ years.
2. There is one question that people have been asking: How is it possible to keep elephants happy _____?
3. Many people who work closely with animals say that they do have _____ and can experience happiness.
4. That means that they live in families and herds and they _____ other elephants.
5. For elephants, communication and social relationships are really _____.

After You Watch

A Discuss these questions with your partner: Have you visited a zoo or seen a video of a zoo? Do you think the animals like living there? Why or why not?

F   Further Practice: *Elephants or People?*

Elephants crossing Luangwa River, Loxodonta africana, Zambia

Listening

A 🔊 11 Listen to the passage. Write numbers to the events in the order they took place.

___ The government made a plan to bring tourists to see the elephants.

___ People built electric fences to stop the elephants.

___ Elephants lived everywhere in Mount Kenya.

___ People came to Mount Kenya and started new farms.

___ People stayed in their farm fields to keep elephants away.

___ Elephants started walking through the farms and destroying them.

___ Farming became easier.

B Match the sentence parts to show the reasons.

1. More people came to Mount Kenya ___
2. Elephants walk through the farms ___
3. The farmers shouted ___
4. The farmers were tired ___
5. Farmers have more time for work now ___
6. The government likes elephants ___

a. because they bring visitors to Kenya.
b. because the fences keep elephants out.
c. because it was elephants' land in the past.
d. because they were scaring elephants all night.
e. because they wanted land for farms.
f. because they wanted the elephants to leave.

C In your opinion, what is the best solution for this elephant problem?

_____
_____

UNIT 4
Life in the Past

The ancient city of Petra, Jordan at night

Look at the photo, then answer the questions:

1 How has life changed over the past 500 years?

2 Which of these changes are the most important to you?

UNIT 4 GOALS

1. Discuss life in the past
2. Contrast different ways of life
3. Compare today with the past
4. Talk about a historical wonder

A GOAL 1: Discuss Life in the Past

▲ Marco Polo

▲ Ibn Battuta

▲ Zheng He

Vocabulary

A Read the information about three early travelers.

Long-distance travel can be difficult for anyone, but it used to be even more challenging. Yet despite the difficulty, people have always wanted to see and learn about distant regions. These three explorers did exactly that—hundreds of years ago! The result was an exchange of knowledge and culture that changed the world.

Marco Polo (1254–1324) We don't know exactly when and where Marco Polo was born, but he lived in Venice and Genoa, in what is now Italy, and he traveled east—far beyond the borders of Europe into Asia. The stories he published after his travels seem to mix together fact and fiction, but they inspired other European explorers, including Christopher Columbus.

Ibn Battuta (1304–1369) Ibn Battuta was a remarkable traveler. Born in Morocco, he visited most of the Muslim world—North Africa, the Middle East, and East Africa—as well as South Asia, including Sri Lanka and India, and even China. Battuta's goal was to search for knowledge and new experiences, and his stories taught people about other parts of the world at a time when few people traveled.

Zheng He (1371–1433) The explorations of Zheng He took him by sea from China to the Middle East and Africa. According to stories, Zheng commanded enormous ships more than 400 feet (122m) long—much, much larger than other ships of the time. The size of the ships was probably helpful for trade, as well as for carrying military people and equipment.

B Write each word in blue next to the correct definition or synonym.

1. _____ was in charge of
2. _____ impressive
3. _____ aim
4. _____ difficult
5. _____ giving and taking
6. _____ travels for discovery
7. _____ far away
8. _____ a type of literature
9. _____ gave enthusiasm or ideas
10. _____ boundary

Word Focus

Use **even though** before a clause with a subject and verb.

Use **despite** before a noun or noun phrase.

They traveled **even though** <u>it was</u> difficult.

They traveled **despite** <u>the difficulty</u>.

Used to

We use *used to* + base form of a verb to talk about the past.	My father **used to** build ships, but now he is retired from his job.
Used to usually shows a contrast between past and present.	The company **used to** publish travel books. (Now they publish cookbooks.)
In questions and negative statements, use *did/didn't* + *use to*.	**Did** people **use to** see pictures of distant places? They **didn't use to** know much about other places and cultures.

A Complete the conversation with the words in the box.

care didn't use
travel used

Sue: Why did people _____ to travel by horse?

Aki: Well, there _____ use to be other transportation.

Sue: OK, but did everyone use to _____ that way?

Aki: Why do you ask? You didn't use to _____ about horses.

Sue: I'm writing about transportation in the past, so I need to include horses.

Aki: You should talk to Mr. Clark. He _____ to ride horses when he was younger, and he knows a lot about them.

Conversation

A 🔊 1 Listen to the conversation and answer the questions.

1. How old are the El Tajín ruins?
   _____

2. What did people use to do there?
   _____

B 🔊 1 Listen to the conversation again and fill in the blanks.

Ben: What's up, Patricia?

Patricia: Not much. I'm _____ of the El Tajín ruins in Mexico.

Ben: I've never _____ El Tajín.

Patricia: It's _____
_____. It has several buildings, some pyramids, ball courts...

Ben: Ball courts? Why are there ball courts?

Patricia: Well, people _____. El Tajín was _____
_____, and the games were part of the culture.

Ben: Ball games? That's interesting!

Patricia: It is, and there are at least _____ on the site!

Ben: Are they used for anything today?

Patricia: Actually, people go to El Tajín now for _____.

▲ El Tajín in Veracruz, Mexico

C 🔁 Practice the conversation with a partner. Then describe the historical places in the box or other places you know about. What used to happen at these places? What happens there now?

The Great Wall in China
Stonehenge in England
The Colosseum in Rome

D 🔁 **GOAL CHECK** ✓ **Discuss life in the past**

How has modern technology changed people's lives? Tell your partner what people used to do in the past, and what they do now. Use the topics in the box and your own ideas.

transportation
communication
home life
entertainment

Unit 4 Life in the Past 49

B GOAL 2: Contrast Different Ways of Life

Listening

A Look at the map on this page. How do you think people used to live in this part of the world 1,000 years ago? Check (✓) the things you think people did.

1. _____ ate fish from the Arctic Ocean
2. _____ lived on small farms
3. _____ followed groups of animals, such as reindeer
4. _____ lived in houses made of wood
5. _____ had their own language and customs

B 🔊 2 Listen to a talk about the Sami people and choose the main idea.

a. The Sami people depend on animals, especially reindeer, to make a living.

b. Life is changing for the Sami people, but some of them live in traditional ways.

c. Many young Sami people want to attend a university and choose a career.

C 🔊 2 Listen again and circle **T** for *true* or **F** for *false*. Correct the false sentences to make them true.

1. Traditionally, the Sami people stayed and lived in one place.   T   F
2. Reindeer were used by the Sami people for food and clothing.   T   F
3. Most Sami people still live in the traditional way.   T   F
4. Some Sami people now raise reindeer on farms.   T   F
5. New laws affect the way Sami people may use land.   T   F

D Do you think it's important to maintain traditions from the past? Or do you think people should focus on the future? Discuss your ideas with a partner.

Word Focus

Some animal words don't have plural forms:

deer   reindeer
sheep   bison

Pronunciation: Reduction of *used to*

When we speak quickly, *used to* is sometimes pronounced /juː-st(ə)/.

A 🔊 **3** You will hear each sentence twice. Listen to the full form and the reduced form of *used to*. Listen again and repeat the sentences.

1. People used to make their own clothes.
2. They used to hunt animals and catch fish.
3. Did you use to play baseball?
4. Food used to cost a lot less.
5. My grandfather used to read to me.

B Complete the sentences with your own information. Then read the sentences aloud to a partner. Use the reduced form /juː-st(ə)/.

1. When I was younger, I used to _____.
2. As a child, I used to want money for _____.
3. In China, people used to _____.
4. Before I was born, my grandparents used to _____.
5. As children, my parents used to _____.

Communication

A How is life today different than it was 50 years ago? Tell your partner at least four things people used to do and what they do now.

> People used to make phone calls at home. Now they use cell phones anywhere.

> True, and their conversations used to be private. Now everyone can hear them!

B How has your life changed over the years? Tell your partner at least four things you didn't use to know or do.

> I didn't use to speak English. Now I speak it every day.

> I didn't use to get along with my brother. Now we're friends.

▲ Old Russian telephone in Norway

C **GOAL CHECK** ✓ **Contrast different ways of life**

Discuss the differences between the traditional Sami lifestyle and the way most Sami people live today. Consider housing, food, education, language, and transportation.

Unit 4 Life in the Past 51

C GOAL 3: Compare Today with the Past

Language Expansion: Separable phrasal verbs

A Some phrasal verbs are used more frequently than one-word verbs. Fill in the blanks with the phrases in the box.

> bring up   help out   turn on   bring back   put on   figure out

Hi, my name is Susie, and I live in the Nunavut Territory in Canada. Life in Nunavut hasn't changed as much as it has in other places. It's true—nowadays, we can _____ the furnace when it gets cold instead of building a fire, but we haven't given up our traditional culture. We still _____ our children in the land our people have lived in for thousands of years. We teach them to _____ our traditional clothing to stay warm in the winter. When they're old enough, we teach them to _____ solutions to everyday problems. We teach them to _____ anything they borrow. And most importantly, we teach them to always _____ their family and their community. Those things will never change.

Word Focus

Separable phrasal verbs can be separated by an object—usually a pronoun.

We **set up** a tent to sleep in.
We **set it up** over there.

B Write the phrasal verbs from Exercise **A** next to the correct synonyms.

1. _____ raise
2. _____ return
3. _____ start
4. _____ discover, solve
5. _____ wear
6. _____ aid

Passive voice in the past

Passive voice in the past	
Use the active voice in the past to focus on the subject of a sentence.	Parents **raised** their children differently in the past.
Use the passive voice in the past to focus on the object or receiver of a past action.	Children **were raised** differently in the past (by their parents).
Form the past passive with *was* or *were* + the past participle of a verb.	My father **was taught** to always tell the truth.

Regular past participles:
invent–invented
pull–pulled
hunt–hunted

Irregular past participles:
eat–eaten
drink–drunk
sell–sold

A Complete each sentence with the past passive form of the verb in parentheses.

1. Large stones _____ (use) to build the Egyptian pyramids.
2. Igloos _____ (build) from blocks of ice by the Inuit people.
3. Writing _____ (invent) in Mesopotamia.
4. Wild animals _____ (hunt) by Native Americans.
5. Chocolate _____ (drink) by the Aztecs.

B How did things get done in the past in China? Complete each sentence with the past passive form of the verb in parentheses and your own ideas.

1. People _____ (tell) about important news by _____.
2. Children _____ (teach) by _____.
3. Clothes _____ (make) by _____.
4. Important books _____ (publish) by _____.
5. People _____ (inspire) by _____.

Conversation

A 4 Close your books and listen to the conversation. What does Luisa want to find out?

▲ An Inuit man builds an igloo.

B 4 Listen to the conversation again and fill in the blanks.

Luisa: Hi, Carl. Can I ask you a question?
Carl: Sure. _____.
Luisa: Do you think _____?
Carl: Of course we do! A lot of important things _____.
Luisa: Like what?
Carl: Well, _____ were developed.
Luisa: OK, those are important. What else?
Carl: A lot of _____ was invented—like the telephone.
Luisa: Yes, that's very important!
Carl: And _____ were made in the past, too.
Luisa: You're right. I do want to know more about the past.
Carl: Good—have fun in your history class!

C Practice the conversation with a partner. Switch roles and practice again. Then make new conversations using your own ideas to answer Luisa's questions.

D GOAL CHECK ✓ **Compare today with the past**

Talk to a partner. How were things done before the following services were developed, and how are they done now?

public transportation   city water systems   garbage collection service

Unit 4 Life in the Past 53

D GOAL 4: Talk About a Historical Wonder

Listening

A What do you know about Genghis Khan? Check (✓) the information you think is true. Compare your answers with your partner's.

_____ He had a difficult childhood.

_____ He was a wise leader and a talented general.

_____ He lived in Central Asia in the eighteenth century.

_____ He conquered many kingdoms and destroyed their cities.

_____ His empire lasted for hundreds of years.

B 🔊 5 Listen to an article and decide whether the following statements are true or false. Circle **T** for *true* or **F** for *false*.

1. After the Mongol attack, Samarkand was a ruined city.   T   F

2. The Mongol Empire covered only a small area.   T   F

3. Modern Mongolians think of Genghis Khan as an important leader.   T   F

4. Genghis Khan became the leader of his people when he was around 40 years old.   T   F

5. People haven't been able to find Genghis Khan's tomb because his soldiers burned it after he was buried.   T   F

C Discuss these questions with a partner. How was Central Asia different after the Mongol Empire? In your opinion, were the changes positive or negative? Give reasons for your answer.

LORD OF THE MONGOLS

Many Mongolians are still nomadic and still live in an easily moveable *ger*.

D GOAL 4: Talk About a Historical Wonder

Taj Mahal in Agra, Uttar Pradesh, India

Bernard Weber wanted to use modern technology to bring the people of the world closer together. He knew that the original Seven Wonders of the Ancient World were chosen by one person, and six of the wonders didn't even exist anymore, so he created a way to let the world determine the New 7 Wonders: an open election using the Internet and text messaging. Anyone could nominate a special site, and anyone could vote.

Millions of votes were cast, and on July 7, 2007, the seven winners were announced in Lisbon, Portugal. They include the Great Wall of China, the Colosseum in Rome, and the Taj Mahal in India. More recently, Weber's Internet-based project has used voting to choose the New 7 Wonders of nature and New 7 Wonders Cities.

Communication

A Discuss the questions with a partner.

1. Which words describe your reaction to historical wonders? Explain your choices and add another word of your own.

   amazed   interested   proud   shocked   inspired   _____

2. Tell your partner about some of the historical wonders from China. What amazing things did people do in the past?

B Read the information in the box about the New 7 Wonders of the World. Choose from the pictures below to create your own version of the New 7 Wonders and give your reasons.

 ▲ Christ Redeemer: Brazil

 ▲ Mount Rushmore: U.S.A.

 ▲ Pyramid of Khufu: Egypt

 ▲ The Great Wall: China

 ▲ Roman Colosseum: Italy

 ▲ Taj Mahal: India

 ▲ Machu Picchu: Peru

 ▲ Petra: Jordan

 ▲ Pyramid at Chichén Itzá: Mexico

VIDEO JOURNAL: *Searching for Genghis Khan* E

Albert Lin in Mongolia

Before You Watch

A Discuss the questions with a partner. Who was Genghis Khan? Where was he from, and why is he famous? Where do people think Genghis Khan is buried? How is Albert Lin going to find his tomb?

B Fill in the blanks with the correct words from the box.

1. Albert Lin is using the most advanced, or _____, technology to find Genghis Khan's tomb.
2. Genghis Khan was buried in a part of Mongolia that is called the _____ Zone, where very few outsiders visit.
3. Because many Mongolians believe Genghis's tomb is _____, or holy, Lin and his team can't dig there.
4. Instead, they are using _____, which detect heat, light, sound, and motion.

> cutting-edge
> Forbidden   sacred
> sensors

While You Watch

A Read the sentences and circle **T** for *true* or **F** for *false*.

1. Albert Lin and his team are working only from the United States to find Genghis's tomb. T F
2. Lin always planned to be an explorer. T F
3. Lin wants to dig up Genghis's tomb and remove the treasure inside. T F
4. Many non-scientists are helping with the research by examining satellite images. T F

After You Watch/Communication

A Make predictions with a partner about how new technology can be used in exploration and research. Think about exploration on land, under the sea, and in space.

Unit 4 Life in the Past 57

F Further Practice: *Living History at Jamestown Settlement*

Listening

A 🔊 6 Listen to the passage and decide the following statements are true or false. Circle **T** for *true* or **F** for *false*.

1. Tourists like to go to Jamestown today. T F
2. In Jamestown, people from three different cultures came together. T F
3. At a living history museum, all of the things to see are inside glass cases. T F
4. Actors work at a living history museum. T F
5. The real ships that the colonists used are in Jamestown. T F
6. You can see a copy of a Native American village in Jamestown. T F
7. The Native Americans around Jamestown didn't know about farming. T F
8. The Jamestown Settlement now is only for learning. T F

B 🔊 6 Which of these things are found in the Jamestown Settlement now? Circle the things that are in the article.

people making pots	actors	archaeologists
people cooking	dogs	people fighting with guns
an old school	staple foods	clothes that people used to wear
ships	a fort	Native American boats

C Answer the questions.

1. Are there any living history museums in China?
   _____
   _____

2. Where are some places that foreign visitors can learn about China's history?
   _____
   _____

D Write about a historical wonder in China. What happened there? What can people see there today?
   _____
   _____
   _____
   _____
   _____

Hans Rosling Professor of Global Health, Co-founder of Gapminder.org

THE MAGIC WASHING MACHINE

Before You Watch

A Look at the picture and answer the questions with a partner.

1. What is this device? Do you have one in your house?
2. What percent of people have a modern washing machine?
3. How has it changed people's lives?

B Here are words you will hear in the TED Talk. Complete the paragraph with the correct words. Not all words will be used.

> **electricity** n. flow of energy used as power
> **heat** v. to cause (something) to become warm or hot
> **load** v. to put (an amount of something) into or onto something
> **mesmerize** v. to hold the attention of (someone) entirely
> **time-consuming** adj. using or needing a large amount of time
> **tough** adj. very difficult to do or deal with

It's amazing how machines can change the world. Not so many years ago, doing laundry was a _____ job. You needed to _____ the water, add

> Hans Rosling's idea worth spreading is that machines have had an incredible effect on the lives of many—and rich westerners can't just tell those in the developing world that they can't have them. Watch Rosling's full TED Talk on TED.com.

the soap and the clothes, and rub them with your hands for a long, long time. Now, we _____ the washing machine, push the button, and the machine does the rest. It's not _____ to get your clothes clean at all. Of course, a washing machine uses _____ to run, and this is a problem as more people get them.

C Look at the pictures on the next page. Check (✓) the information that you predict you will hear in the TED Talk.

___ 1. Doing laundry is usually work for women and girls.
___ 2. People in rich countries have a lot of different machines in their homes.
___ 3. We should drive less and walk or ride bikes more.

While You Watch

A Watch the TED Talk. Circle the main idea.

1. Washing machines are very popular around the world.
2. Women like to read more than they like to do laundry.
3. When people don't have to do so much hard work, they have time to do things they enjoy and their lives change in positive ways.

TED TALKS

B ▶ The images below relate to the TED Talk. Watch the TED Talk again and write the letter of the caption under the correct photo.

a. Women in Sweden used to wash clothes by hand.
b. People in developed countries use half of the world's energy.
c. Having a washing machine gave Rosling's mother time to read.

1. ____

2. ____

3. ____

Challenge! What would happen if all families around the world could use a modern washing machine? What would be the benefits and the challenges? What does Rosling think we should do about the challenges? Share your ideas with the class. Give reasons for your opinions.

"Because this is the magic: you load the laundry, and what do you get out of the machine? You get books out of the machines, children's books. And mother got time to read for me."

—Hans Rosling

Hans Rosling Professor of Global Health, Co-founder of Gapminder.org
THE MAGIC WASHING MACHINE

After You Watch

A Complete the summary with the words in the box.

| developing | education | improves | researches | washing |

Hans Rosling _____ how people live around the world. He believes that by reducing hard work, like _____ clothes by hand, women and girls in _____ countries will have more time to read and study. Why is that important? Because when people have an _____, their quality of life _____.

B Match the phrases to state information from the TED Talk.

____ 1. number of people in the world   a. 22%
____ 2. amount the richest people spend daily b. $2
____ 3. current total energy consumption   c. 7 billion
____ 4. amount the poorest people spend daily d. $80
____ 5. future total energy consumption   e. 12%

C Read the statements below. Circle the ones that paraphrase Hans Rosling's opinions.

1. People in rich countries use much of the energy in the world.
2. Most people in the world are not very poor.
3. People who use a lot of energy shouldn't tell other people not to.
4. Getting a washing machine made a big difference in his family's life.
5. We should not have more technology in the world.

Project

Hans Rosling believes that small transitions in individual lives can make a big difference in the world. As people move out of poverty and do less time-consuming work, they gain time to get an education and find better jobs. Use his ideas to survey your classmates about an important transition for people in China.

In many developing countries, women do the hard work of carrying water.

A Look at the list of devices. Circle the two you think have made the biggest difference in people's lives in the last century.

| microwave oven | vacuum cleaner | air conditioner |
| computer | cell phone | dishwasher |

B Compare your choices in Exercise **A** with your partner's. Are there any devices you'd like to add to the list? Think about devices that save on work and give people more time to read and get an education.

C Take a survey. Write a question for each item. Ask each question and then ask a follow-up question for details. Use the chart to take notes.

	Question	Name	Details
1. most expensive			
2. most useful at home			
3. helped the most people			
4. caused the biggest problems			
5. caused the most pollution			

> What's the most important device in the 21st century?
>
> I think it's the cell phone.
>
> Why do you think that?

Presentation Strategy

Using numbers to support facts

Hans Rosling uses numbers and statistics to surprise the audience and support his argument in interesting and humorous ways.

Challenge! Hans Rosling is interested in the differences between what we think we know about the world and the way things really are. He's also very curious about the ways the world is going to change. Go to TED.com and find another TED Talk by Hans Rosling. What has he learned, and what predictions does he make?

UNIT 5

Careers

Photographer working off the shores of Dominica

Look at the photo, then answer the questions:

1. What is the person in the picture doing?
2. What knowledge and skills does this person have?

UNIT 5 GOALS

1. Discuss career choices
2. Ask and answer job-related questions
3. Talk about career planning
4. Talk about innovative jobs

A GOAL 1: Discuss Career Choices

Vocabulary

A 🔊 1 Listen to a conversation between a high school senior and a career advisor. What does Marcy do at the hospital?

B 🔊 1 Listen again. Then fill in the blanks in Ms. Carter's notes below with the words in the box.

> employee   experience   owner   assistant
> training   qualifications   volunteer   boss

- Marcy has some work _____. She went through a _____ program to become a family _____ at the hospital. It's _____ work, so Marcy doesn't get paid.

- Marcy would like to be a business _____, but she doesn't have the necessary _____ yet.

- I explained that she could start as an _____ at a business. Later, perhaps, she can be the _____ when she has her own business.

C 👥 Talk in pairs. What do you think Marcy should do to prepare for her future? Did the advisor give her good advice?

Modals for giving advice

Modals for giving advice	
Use modals of advice to talk about what is or isn't a good idea. Modals are followed by the simple form of a verb.	You **should** <u>choose</u> a career that fits your personality. Miguel **ought to** <u>become</u> an engineer. Linda **shouldn't** <u>take</u> that office job.
Had better is stronger than *should* or *ought to*. It means something bad could happen if the advice isn't followed.	You **had better** <u>talk</u> to the academic advisor before you decide on a major. I**'d better not** <u>miss</u> any more days of work.
Use *maybe*, *perhaps*, or *I think* with modals to make the advice sound gentler and friendlier.	**Maybe** you **should** <u>become</u> a health care worker.

A Complete the sentences with a partner. Use your own ideas.

> **Career Advice**
> - If you want to become a successful businessperson, you should _____, but you shouldn't _____.
> - If you really like animals, you ought to _____.
> - When you go for a job interview, you had better _____, and you had better not _____. Good luck!

B Read one of the problems out loud to a partner. Your partner will give you friendly advice using *maybe, perhaps*, or *I think*.

1. My school is far from my house.
2. I think I may be getting sick.
3. I want to become a doctor.
4. My job doesn't pay very well.
5. My university application was rejected.
6. I never remember my mother's birthday.

> **I don't get along with my co-worker.**
>
> **Maybe you should avoid him.**

Conversation

A Close your book and listen to the conversation. Why doesn't Bob like his job?

B Listen to the conversation again and fill in the blanks.

Miranda: Hi Bob. How's it going?
Bob: Not so good. I think _____.
Miranda: _____. What is it you do again?
Bob: I'm _____. That's like a secretary, but _____.
Miranda: Do you have a good boss?
Bob: Sure. He's the owner of the company, _____, actually.
Miranda: So what's the problem? Is it the other people you work with?
Bob: No, my co-workers are fine, but _____.
Miranda: Maybe you should start looking for _____.
Bob: You're right. I can probably find something better.

C Practice the conversation with a partner. Then have new conversations about problems that might be nice to have; for example:

I make too much money.   **I have too much vacation time.**

D GOAL CHECK ✓ **Discuss career choices**

Work in pairs. Choose a career from the box and describe the training, experience, and other qualifications required for that career. Then talk about the advantages and disadvantages of having that career.

Business:
accountant, salesperson, sales representative
Computers:
system analyst, web designer, software engineer, information technology specialist
Education:
principal, teacher
Entertainment:
actor, musician
Health:
dentist, doctor, nurse, health care worker
Tourism:
hotel manager, travel agent, tour guide
Others:
lawyer, engineer

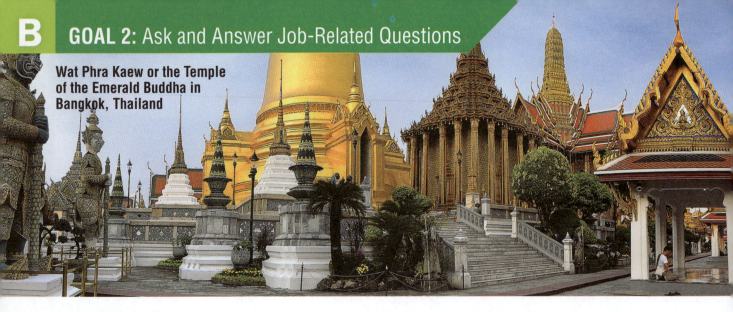

B GOAL 2: Ask and Answer Job-Related Questions

Wat Phra Kaew or the Temple of the Emerald Buddha in Bangkok, Thailand

Engage!

Is it better to be a business owner or an employee?

Listening

A 🔊 3 Listen to an interview with a restaurant owner. Why did he start his own business?

B 🔊 3 Listen again and answer the questions.

1. When did Mr. Sangumram open the New Thailand restaurant? _____
2. Who is the cook at the restaurant? _____
3. What kind of food is served at the restaurant? _____
4. How far from the owner's home is the restaurant? _____
5. How many employees work at the restaurant? _____
6. What does Mr. Sangumram's wife do for a living? _____

C What makes a good job? Rank the following from 1 (most important) to 6 (least important). Share your answers with a partner.

____ amount of vacation time   ____ distance from home
____ wage or salary level   ____ long-term employment
____ working alone or with others   ____ interesting job duties

Pronunciation

In *yes/no* questions, the speaker's voice rises on the last content word.

Did you talk to your boss?   **Is she going to pay you a higher salary?**

In questions with *wh-* words, we use a rising then falling intonation over the last content word.

When is your job interview?   **What qualifications do you need?**

A Imagine you are applying for a job at Mr. Sangumram's restaurant. He needs a waiter, a dishwasher, and an assistant cook. Which job would you apply for? Write questions about the job with a partner.

Yes/No questions	Wh- questions
Is the restaurant open late at night?	What are the job duties?
_____	_____
_____	_____
_____	_____

B Join another pair of students and role-play a job interview. Ask the other pair your questions from Exercise **A**. They will answer using their own ideas.

Communication

A Read the career profiles on the right. Choose two careers that might be good for you, but don't tell anyone which jobs you chose.

B Ask your partner several questions about the kind of career he or she might want in the future. Then try to guess which two careers your partner chose.

> Do you like to work outdoors?

> How much do you know about medications?

C GOAL CHECK ✓ Ask and answer job-related questions

Join another pair of students. Ask each other questions and decide which career is best for each person in the group.

Career Profiles

Commercial Pilot: Knows about airplane mechanics, weather, radio communication. Works long hours. Often far away from home.

Pharmacist: Knows about medications. Advises patients about their treatments. Long-term employment. Some vacation time.

Diving Instructor: Understands and teaches the use of scuba equipment. Works outdoors. Should be a strong swimmer. Salary varies by season.

Retail Sales Clerk: Manages store merchandise. Assists customers. Should be able to work with others and stand for several hours at a time.

C GOAL 3: Talk About Career Planning

Language Expansion: Participial adjectives

A 🔊 4 Listen to the passage and choose the best answer to finish each of the following statements.

1. A. J. Coston is now _____.
   a. a college student
   b. a firefighter
   c. a weekend volunteer
   d. an emergency worker

2. A. J. Coston is interested in firefighting because _____.
   a. his mother is a firefighter
   b. he was saved once by a firefighter
   c. his friends are interested in it, too
   d. this has been his dream job

> That was relaxing. Now I feel relaxed.

> I think you went to a park.

Word Focus

Participial Adjectives

That was _____.
Now I feel _____.

relaxing/relaxed
embarrassing/embarrassed
tiring/tired
confusing/confused
disappointing/disappointed
exciting/excited
depressing/depressed

B 🔊 4 Listen to the passage again and fill in each blank with the exact word you hear.

A. J. Coston isn't waiting to start his dream job. At age 18, he's a weekend volunteer firefighter in the United States. During the week, he lives at home with his mom, dad, and sister, and does his main job: going to high school. "I always wanted to get into firefighting since I was a little kid watching fire trucks go by," he says. "One day I was _____ and on the Internet, and I found out that Loudoun County offered a junior firefighter program."

Some of A. J.'s friends are _____ by his decision to spend weekends at the firehouse, but to A. J., helping people is more _____ than anything else. The job is never _____, either, since firefighters get called to all sorts of emergencies. One _____ moment for A. J. was getting an emergency call after four children were struck by lightning. Luckily, all four survived.

A. J. will be off to college next fall, and plans to study what he's most _____ in: emergency medical care. "I want to be a flight medic on a helicopter eventually," he says.

C ♻ For each participial adjective you fill in the blank above, decide whether it describes (1) someone's feelings or (2) something that causes a certain feeling. Then practice the sentences in the Word Focus box with a partner.

D ♻ Two kindergarten teachers are talking. Complete their conversation with -ing and -ed adjectives made from words in the box.

> bore   surprise   satisfy   terrify   interest   tire

Adam: So how was your first day?

Cassie: It was great! I felt so nervous at first; I was really _____. But after that, I enjoyed it. The kids are great.

Adam: What did you do with them?

Cassie: First, they drew pictures, and then they told stories about the pictures. The stories were so _____ that I wanted to write them down!

Adam: Did the head teacher come to see your class?

Cassie: Yes, he did, and he was very pleased. He said I'm doing well. I was really _____. I thought I would have a lot of problems, but it went very well.

Adam: Teaching young children is really _____ because they learn so fast.

Cassie: I'm sure I'll never be _____, but teaching kids is very _____. I'm ready to go to sleep already!

Conversation

A 🔊 5 Listen to the conversation. Circle **T** for *true* or **F** for *false*.

1. Kimberly knows what he wants to do after graduation.   **T**   **F**
2. Parker plans to be a car dealer.   **T**   **F**
3. The training program can offer Parker a job.   **T**   **F**
4. Kimberly will start planning soon.   **T**   **F**

B 🔊 5 Listen to the conversation again and fill in the blanks.

Parker: Hi, Kimberly. What do you want to do _____?

Kimberly: I'm not sure, but I want to _____.

Parker: Of course! Everybody wants that, but _____.

Kimberly: OK, what are you planning to do when you finish school?

Parker: I'm planning to _____. They teach you _____.

Kimberly: You sound excited about that.

Parker: I am! You know I've always loved cars, and _____, so I can get a job really soon.

Kimberly: That sounds great! I need to start thinking about my future, too.

Parker: Mmm hmm. That's what I said before.

Kimberly: And you're right, _____.

C Practice the conversation with a partner. Switch roles and practice it again. Make a new conversation using your own plans for the future.

D GOAL CHECK ✓ **Talk about career planning**

Talk to a partner. What kind of career would be interesting and satisfying to you? What are you doing now to prepare for your future career?

Unit 5 Careers   71

D GOAL 4: Talk About Innovative Jobs

Listening

A What jobs do you think of as especially innovative? Look at the list below or come up with your own ideas. Share them with a partner.

| salesclerk | lawyer | inventor | bus driver |
| designer | researcher | programmer | travel photographer |

B 🔊 6 Listen to the passage. Complete the sentences with the correct words in parentheses.

1. Pritchard was _____ (happy | angry) when he got his idea for the water purifier.
2. Pritchard works _____ (at home | in a laboratory).
3. He believes that "old thinking" needs to _____ (continue | change).
4. Many people have to _____ (buy | boil) their water before they drink it.
5. Lifesaver water purifiers are very _____ (efficient | expensive).

C 🔊 6 Listen to the passage again and choose the best answer to finish each of the following statements.

1. In the two disasters mentioned in the passage, it took _____ before people could drink safe drinking water.
   a. one or two months
   b. a year
   c. a few days
   d. eighteen months

2. Pritchard looked for different solutions because he thought the traditional way was _____.
   a. difficult to use
   b. not safe to use
   c. not effective
   d. more expensive to operate

3. Which statement about water poverty is right according to the passage?
   a. The main reason for it is natural disasters.
   b. About one seventh of the world population suffer from it.
   c. It makes poorer people poorer.
   d. It prevents children from going to school.

4. According to Pritchard, with the water purifying bottle, people living in areas suffering from water poverty will _____.
   a. enjoy better community life
   b. find treatment to some diseases
   c. have a lower death rate
   d. use more fossil fuels

D List two problems that drinking unsafe water causes. Compare your answers with your partner's. How does the water purifying bottle help?

TED Ideas worth spreading

Michael Pritchard Inventor, Problem Solver

MAKING FILTHY WATER DRINKABLE

"I'd like to show you that through thinking differently, the problem has been solved."

— Michael Pritchard

Michael Pritchard's idea worth spreading is that everyone should have access to clean water—and here's a way to give it to them. Watch Pritchard's full TED Talk on TED.com.

D GOAL 4: Talk About Innovative Jobs

An employee shows a powerful new computer that will be able to handle the large amount of calculations needed for nano technology research.

---

community-based conservation
developing world
food systems
undersea exploration
endangered species
non-profit organization

For Your Information
What is an advice column?

An advice column is a column traditionally presented in a magazine or newspaper, though it can also be delivered through other news media, such as the Internet and broadcast news media. The advice column format is question and answer: a (usually anonymous) reader writes to the media outlet with a problem in the form of a question, and the media outlet provides an answer or response. The responses are written by an advice columnist (colloquially known in British English as an agony aunt, or agony uncle if the columnist is male).

—from Wikipedia

Communication

A What other innovators do you know? Look at the other TED readings and TED Talks. What makes them innovators? Use the ideas in the box.

B | GOAL CHECK ✓ **Talk about innovative jobs**

Share your ideas about innovators. What do they have in common?

Activity

A Suppose you are working in the team of Ann Landers, the Advice Columnist. Now you are giving advice orally in response to Mr. White's question: "How to become an innovator?" Use **should**, **had better**, or **ought to**.

> **Modals for giving advice**
>
> English uses a variety of modals for giving advice, and choosing the correct one requires being sensitive to the relationship between the speakers. *Had better* and *had better not* imply a relationship of authority (such as a boss, teacher, or doctor). *Should* and *ought* to are more neutral, but native speakers usually try to soften their advice by adding *I think* or *maybe*, especially when speaking with friends.

You may use the following outline:

   Mr. White, thank you for your letter asking for advice on how to become an innovator. In your letter, you said _____ and _____ (the reader's background information: age, gender, career, etc.).

   In my opinion, an innovator _____, and _____. He / She _____ (not).

   So you _____ and you _____ (not).
You _____.

   At last, I hope my advice can help you get closer to your dream.

   Best regards.

VIDEO JOURNAL: *Trinidad Bird Man* E

The scarlet ibis is the national bird of Trinidad and Tobago.

Before You Watch

A Complete the sentences with a word from the box.

1. A _____ is a very tiny bird.
2. An _____ studies birds.
3. _____ is a place where everything is beautiful, delightful, and peaceful.
4. Panda bears, honeybees, and dolphins are all examples of _____.
5. A _____ is a home that birds build for themselves.

wildlife   hummingbird
paradise   nest
ornithologist

While You Watch

A ▶ Watch the video *Trinidad Bird Man*. Check (✓) Roger Neckles's job qualifications in the box on the right.

☐ He enjoys being outdoors.
☐ He can take photographs.
☐ He doesn't mind a low salary.
☐ He's very patient.
☐ He's enthusiastic about birds.
☐ He's an excellent writer.

After You Watch/Communication

A Interview a partner and write down his or her answers in your notebook.

1. What time do you like to get up in the morning?
2. How do you feel about spending a lot of time outdoors?
3. Are you a very patient person? Why or why not?
4. Do you prefer to wear casual clothes or stylish clothes?
5. What do you think is the most interesting kind of wildlife?

B Should your partner become a wildlife photographer? Tell the class why or why not.

> You should become a _____ because...

Unit 5 Careers   75

F Further Practice: *Dream Jobs: Mona Davis*

Listening

A Guess what you will hear with the following key words.

movie critic	rating	review
qualification	filmmaking	filmmaker

B 🔊 7 Listen to a passage and complete the following chart with your own words.

Name	
Job	
Qualifications	
Job duties	watch write
Good things about job	can see can help
Bad things about job	sometimes feels people

C Is Mona's job a dream job for you? Explain your answer.

___

D Talk about someone who has a great job. Write down a few key points including: Who is the person? Why is it a great job? What are this person's job duties? How did this person become qualified for the job?

___

Unit 5 Careers

UNIT 6
Celebrations

Carnival is celebrated in towns and villages throughout Brazil. Rio de Janeiro is the Carnival Capital of the World.

Look at the photo, then answer the questions:

1. What is your favorite celebration?
2. What do people do there?

UNIT 6 GOALS

1. Describe a festival
2. Compare holidays in different countries
3. Talk about celebrations
4. Share opinions about holidays

A GOAL 1: Describe a Festival

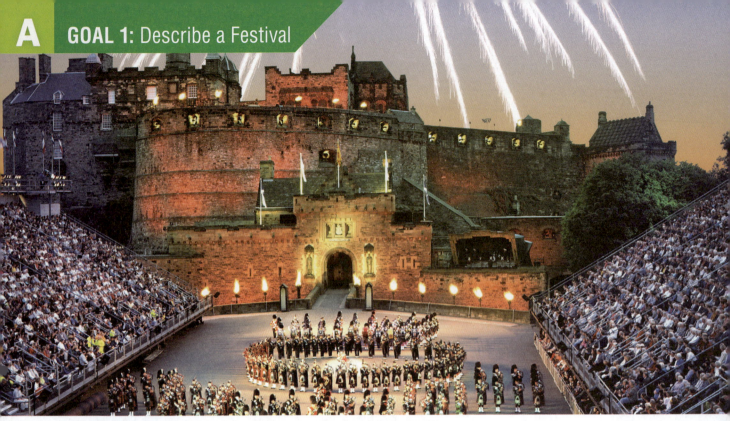

▲ Hogmanay celebration in Scotland

Vocabulary

A 🔊 1 Listen to the passage about a special New Year's celebration and fill in the blanks.

> New Year's Day is a holiday around the world, but people in Edinburgh, Scotland, _____ it in an exciting way. They have a _____ called Hogmanay. Hogmanay _____ all around the city, from December 29 to January 1. It starts with a _____ on the night of December 29. On December 30, there are _____ and dancing. Finally, on New Year's Eve, there is a street party with fireworks, and people wear very colorful _____. There is always a big _____ even though it's very cold. One year, more than 100,000 people _____. The celebration in Edinburgh is very _____, but the _____ Hogmanay festivals in other cities in Scotland are popular, too.

B Write the exact words in the passage next to the correct meaning.

1. _____ performances given by musicians or singers
2. _____ famous
3. _____ procession of people or things
4. _____ large group of people
5. _____ happening once each year
6. _____ special clothes for a performance
7. _____ an event with performances of music, etc.
8. _____ do something enjoyable for a special day

Engage!

How do you celebrate New Year's Day?

C Discuss these questions with a partner. What festivals have you participated in? What festivals do you know about? Would you like to participate in Hogmanay in Edinburgh? Why or why not?

Conversation

A 2 Close your book and listen to the conversation. When is the festival they talk about?

B 2 Listen to the conversation again, and fill in the blanks with the exact words you hear.

Dave: Yuki, are there any special festivals in your city?

Yuki: Oh, _____! My favorite is called *Setsubun*.

Dave: Really? What's that?

Yuki: Well, it takes place in February. _____.

Dave: What do you do then?

Yuki: _____, and they say "_____!" Then _____. And there are lots of parties.

Dave: That sounds like fun.

Yuki: It is!

C Practice the conversation with a partner. Then have new conversations about your favorite holidays and celebrations.

D GOAL CHECK ✓ **Describe a festival**

Talk to a partner about a special festival in your city. Tell your partner when, why, and how you celebrate this festival.

▲ Setsubun procession in Tokyo

Unit 6 Celebrations 81

B GOAL 2: Compare Holidays in Different Countries

Day of the Dead

Country: _____

When is it? _____

How do people celebrate it?

a. go to the cemetery with _____

b. bring _____

What is the special food?

a. sweet _____

b. shaped like skulls _____

Listening

A 🔊 3 Listen to three people talk about a holiday in their country. Number the countries in the order that you hear about them.

　　a. Japan _____　　b. Mexico _____　　c. United States _____

B 🔊 3 Listen again and fill in the charts.

Halloween

Country: _____
When is it? _____
How do people celebrate it?
a. put on _____
b. ask for _____
c. watch _____
What is the special food?
a. _____
b. _____

O-Bon

Country: _____
When is it? _____
How do people celebrate it?
a. go back to _____
b. participate in a special _____
c. make big _____

C Discuss these questions with a partner.

1. Do you know about any other holidays like this?
2. Why do you think different countries have similar holidays?

Pronunciation: Question intonation with lists

A 4 Listen to the questions. Notice how the intonation rises and falls in questions with a list of choices.

1. Would you like cake, ↗ ice cream, ↗ or fruit? ↘
2. Is O-Bon in July ↗ or August? ↘

B 5 Read the questions and mark the intonation with arrows. Then listen and check your answers.

1. Do you have special food at breakfast, lunch, or dinner?
2. Have you celebrated New Year's in France, Australia, or both?
3. Is your costume red or pink?
4. Is O-Bon in August or September?
5. Do you celebrate with dancing, singing, or gift-giving?

C Say each question from Exercise **B** to your partner. Give each other feedback on your pronunciation.

Communication

A Imagine that your group can take a trip to participate in one of the holidays in Exercise **A** on Page 82. Discuss these questions. Then explain your group's final decision to the class.

1. How are these holidays similar? Think of as many answers as you can.
2. How are they different?
3. What could visitors do at each holiday?
4. Which holiday would you like to participate in? Why?

B **GOAL CHECK** ✓ **Compare holidays in different countries**

Take turns. Tell a partner how the different groups' trips will be similar and how they will be different.

C GOAL 3: Talk About Celebrations

Baseball team celebrates after a win.

Language Expansion: Expressions for celebrations

A Read the following expressions, and discuss the occasions on which they may be used.

Expressions	Occasions
Congratulations!	
Well-done!	
Thanks for having invited/inviting us!	
Good luck!	
Happy anniversary / birthday / New Year!	

B Write the correct expression for each situation.

1. You're leaving someone's house after a dinner party. _____
2. Your friend has to take a difficult exam tomorrow. _____
3. Your neighbor tells you he plans to get married soon. _____
4. Today is your friend's birthday. You see your friend. _____
5. Your friend got an excellent grade on an exam. _____

C What do people usually do to celebrate the following occasions?

1. Birthday
2. Thanksgiving Day
3. Christmas
4. Wedding anniversary
5. Graduation ceremony

Would rather

Use *would rather* + base form of the verb to talk about actions we prefer or like more than other actions.	**I would rather go** to a big wedding than go to a small wedding.
We often use a contraction of *would*.	**They'd rather meet** us at the library.
Use *would rather not* + base form of the verb to talk about things we don't want to do.	**She'd rather not go** to the meeting. It's going to be long and boring.
Use *would rather* + base form of the verb in *yes/no* questions to ask people about their preferences.	**Would you rather have** the dinner party at our house or at a restaurant?

Conversation

A 🔊 6 Close your book and listen to the conversation. What will they probably do to celebrate New Year's Eve?

B 🔊 6 Listen to the conversation again, and fill in the blanks with the exact words you hear.

Mike: New Year's Eve is next week. What would you like to do?

Katie: Let's _____!

Mike: I'd rather _____ and _____.

Katie: That's boring! We could _____. Or would you rather _____?

Mike: I'd rather _____. It's always so noisy and crowded.

Katie: I have an idea. Let's _____ and _____.

Mike: That sounds like a better plan.

C Practice the conversation with a partner. Switch roles and practice it again.

D Make notes. What do you usually do to celebrate these days?

	Your birthday	Your favorite holiday: _____
When is it?		
Where do you celebrate it?		
How do you celebrate it?		
What are the special foods?		

E Work with a partner. Make plans to celebrate one of these days together.

F GOAL CHECK ✓ **Talk about celebrations**

Join another pair of students and share your plans.

Unit 6 Celebrations

D GOAL 4: Share Opinions About Holidays

Listening

A Discuss these questions with a partner.
1. What are the most important holidays in China?
2. Are they new or old? How did they start?

B 🔊 7 Listen to the passage and fill in the missing information.
1. the number of people who celebrate Kwanzaa now _____
2. the dates of Kwanzaa _____
3. the year when Kwanzaa started _____
4. three countries where people celebrate Kwanzaa _____
5. the most important symbol of Kwanzaa _____
6. the colors of Kwanzaa _____

C 🔊 7 Listen to the passage again. Then circle **T** for *true*, **F** for *false*.

1. Kwanzaa is celebrated at the end of the year.   T   F
2. Kwanzaa is a holiday for African Americans.   T   F
3. Kwanzaa is a very old holiday.   T   F
4. People spend a lot of time with their families during Kwanzaa. T   F
5. Children receive presents at the end of Kwanzaa.   T   F
6. Everyone thinks Kwanzaa is an important holiday.   T   F

STARTING A NEW TRADITION

D GOAL 4: Share Opinions About Holidays

Chuseok celebration in Korea

| I agree. |
| I'm not sure. |
| I disagree. |

Communication

A Express your opinion about these sentences. Use the expressions in the box.

1. A new holiday isn't a real holiday.
2. Some old holidays are not very important now.
3. China should start a new holiday.
4. People spend too much money for holidays.
5. It's very important to keep all of the old holiday customs.

Speaking Strategy:
An effective opinion paragraph

1. Begin with a strong topic sentence which clearly states your point of view.

2. Support your opinion by giving good, logical reasons for it.

3. End with a brief conclusion related to the opinion and reasons you gave.

B Choose one of the statements from Exercise **A**, and draft a longer opinion to be presented orally. Be sure the opinion paragraph contains all three elements from the "Speaking Strategy".

C GOAL CHECK ✓ Share opinions about holidays

Compare your opinion with your partner's. The following questions can help you check the structure of the opinion paragraph.

1. Does the paragraph have a strong, clear topic sentence? Explain.
2. Is your partner's opinion supported with good reasons? Explain.
3. Is there a conclusion that ends the paragraph well? Explain.

D Think about a holiday you don't enjoy. What do people usually do during the holiday? What would you rather do?

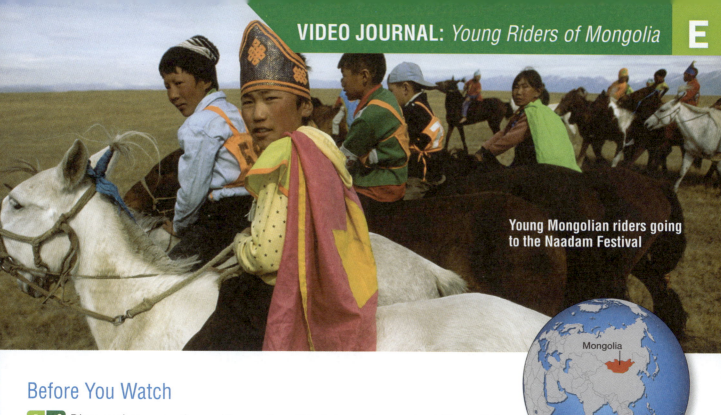

VIDEO JOURNAL: Young Riders of Mongolia E

Young Mongolian riders going to the Naadam Festival

Before You Watch

A Discuss these questions with a partner. What do you know about Mongolia? Have you ever seen a horse race? Describe what you saw.

While You Watch

A Watch the video *Young Riders of Mongolia*. Write two unusual things about the Naadam horse race.

1. _____   2. _____

B Watch the video again. Circle **T** for *true* or **F** for *false*.

1. In Mongolia today, people ride horses only for special celebrations.   T   F
2. The Naadam Festival celebrates traditional sports.   T   F
3. The Naadam horse race is very short.   T   F
4. People want to get close to the horses for good luck.   T   F
5. The winning horses get a lot of money.   T   F

After You Watch/Communication

A Discuss these questions in a small group. What are some traditional sports in China? Are they still popular?

B Create a festival to introduce foreigners to the culture of China. Present your festival to the class.

- Give the festival a name.
- Think of three sports, foods, and shows that will be in the festival.
- Make a poster to advertise your festival.

Unit 6 Celebrations 89

F Further Practice: *The Oldest Celebration in the World*

Listening

A 🔊 8 Listen to the passage "The Oldest Celebration in the World" and circle **T** for *true* or **F** for *false*.

1. Midsummer celebrates the most difficult time of the year.	T	F
2. Midsummer is the shortest night of the year.	T	F
3. In the past, Midsummer was an important holiday for farmers.	T	F
4. Midsummer fires were a symbol of the sun.	T	F
5. Midsummer customs are the same in all countries.	T	F
6. Now, Midsummer is mostly a holiday for having fun.	T	F

B 🔊 8 Listen to the passage again. Then circle the places where people do these things for Midsummer. Some places may be used more than once.

1. eat special food	Sweden	Finland	Spain
2. have parties	Sweden	Finland	Spain
3. go to the beach	Sweden	Finland	Spain
4. try to find out about the future	Sweden	Finland	Spain
5. do special things for their health	Sweden	Finland	Spain
6. celebrate at night	Sweden	Finland	Spain

C Make an advertisement for a celebration in your city.

Come and celebrate _____ with us! It's well known because _____. You'll see colorful _____. You can participate in _____. The _____ is/are exciting. It's as _____ as _____. It takes place _____. Don't miss it!

Beverly and Dereck Joubert Documentary Filmmakers/ Conservationists, National Geographic Explorers-in-Residence
LIFE LESSONS FROM BIG CATS

A Look at the picture and answer the questions with a partner.

1. What kind of animal is in the photo?
2. Where do these animals live?
3. What else do you know about these animals and their habitat?

B Look at the words in the box. Complete the paragraph with the correct word. Not all words will be used.

> **collectively** *adj.* shared or done by a group of people
> **condone** *v.* to allow (something that is considered wrong) to continue
> **crash** *v.* to go down very suddenly and quickly
> **disrupt** *v.* to cause (something) to be unable to continue in the normal way
> **pride** *n.* a group of lions
> **revenue stream** *n.* a flow of money that is made by or paid to a business or an organization

Africa's big cats are endangered, and we are all _____ responsible. Soon, the _____ of lions may disappear. Because we _____ hunting and other activities that put them at risk, their numbers have _____ in the last 50 years. And it's not only the big cats that are in danger—ecotourism brings in a large _____ to Africa. If the cats disappear, so will the money and jobs.

Beverly and Dereck Jouberts' idea worth spreading is that not only do big cats like lions and leopards have big personalities, but getting to know them can help protect Africa. Watch the Jouberts' full TED Talk on TED.com.

C Beverly and Dereck Joubert are wildlife photographers who publicize the problem of endangered big cats. What do you predict you will hear in their TED Talk? Look at the pictures on the next page. Check (✓) the information you predict you will hear.

_____ 1. They have spent five years watching a leopard cub grow up.

_____ 2. They are also researching the behavior of giraffes and elephants.

_____ 3. Their investigations have shown that these lions are essential.

_____ 4. Lion bones are being sold.

TEDTALKS

While You Watch

A ▶ Watch the TED Talk. Circle the main idea.

1. It's necessary to study big cats over many years.
2. If the big cats disappear, many other species may disappear.
3. Beverly and Dereck Joubert believe that big cats are beautiful.

B ▶ Watch the TED Talk again and match the photo that illustrates the TED Talk to the correct caption.

_____ a. If a male lion is killed, the members of his pride may also die.

_____ b. The Jouberts have discovered that some lions hunt in the water.

_____ c. Legadema trusts the Jouberts and lets them come close to her.

_____ d. The Jouberts have studied a young leopard named Legadema since she was a baby.

1.

2.

3.

4.

"And I know, in the light of human suffering and poverty and even climate change, one would wonder, why worry about a few cats?"

– Beverly Joubert

Beverly and Derek Joubert Documentary Filmmakers/Conservationists, National Geographic Explorers-in-Residence

LIFE LESSONS FROM BIG CATS

After You Watch

A Complete the summary with the words in the box.

| extinction | passionate | photographing | respect | survive |

Beverly and Dereck Joubert are _____ about protecting the African wilderness. They have spent many years studying and _____ big cats. In the last 50 years, these cats have been pushed to the edge of _____ by hunters. The Jouberts believe that if the big cats are viewed with _____, they can survive. And if the big cats _____, they can help us maintain our connection to nature and to other human beings.

B Match the phrases to the information from the video.

____ 1. number of lions alive now   a. $80 billion
____ 2. number of leopards left in the wild b. 5
____ 3. years the Jouberts have been filming big cats c. 20,000
____ 4. revenue stream from ecotourism   d. 50,000
____ 5. number of years the Jouberts followed Legadema e. 28

C Read the statements below. Circle the ones that paraphrase information in the TED Talk.

1. Many kinds of big cats live in the African wilderness.
2. It's important to protect big cats and the humans who live near them.
3. There used to be more than 450,000 lions in Africa.
4. It is wrong to hunt and kill lions for sport.
5. If we aren't connected to nature, we will lose hope.

Project

Beverly and Dereck Joubert want to protect the African wilderness. Use their ideas to write a letter in support of big cat conservation to the editor of a newspaper. Follow these steps.

A Work with a partner to find facts and opinions from the TED Talk that you can include. Complete the chart below. Choose the ones that support your idea the best.

FACT	OPINION

B Write your letter. Use the frame below to organize your ideas. Then show your letter to a different partner. Is your opinion easy to understand? Does he or she have ideas for improvement?

To the Editor:

I am writing to _____. In my opinion, _____. If we don't _____, we will _____. It is also important to _____. We will _____ if we _____.

Finally, I think _____. If _____, then _____.

Yours sincerely,

_____

Challenge! Beverly and Dereck Joubert are working to ensure the long-term survival of big cats. Find out more about the Big Cats Initiative at TED.com and explore ways you can get involved. Share what you learn with the class.

UNIT 7
The Mind

An Eastern screech owl in its nest

Look at the photo, then answer the questions:

1 What can you see in the picture?

2 Why is it difficult to see the image?

UNIT 7 GOALS

1. Talk about learning strategies
2. Talk about your senses
3. Talk about your fears
4. Describe an emotional experience

A GOAL 1: Talk About Learning Strategies

▲ Taxi in London, England

Vocabulary

A 🔊 1 Listen to the passage and fill in the blanks.

A Bigger Brain

Every day, Glen McNeil rides his motorbike around London for seven hours. He wants to become a taxi driver, so he must _____ every street in the city and then pass a test called "The Knowledge of London." He will answer questions about 400 routes between important places. It's an incredible test of memory. The examiner names two places, and candidates must _____ quickly and give the names of every street and _____ along the route between those two places.

Preparing for the exam takes three years, and passing it is extremely difficult. Some people try as many as twelve times. McNeill uses many different _____ for studying at home. He _____ all the places on a route to make a _____ map. He also concentrates on _____ street names that sound similar.

Now scientists have discovered important differences in these drivers' brains. The _____ of the brain that _____ information about places is larger in London taxi drivers than in other people. Learning "The Knowledge" might make their brains grow new _____ .

a. ways of doing an activity
b. learn to remember exactly
c. microscopic part of the body
d. make a picture in your mind
e. remembering
f. keep, continue to have
g. part
h. in your mind
i. respond
j. outstanding building or other feature

B Match the following words with their meanings in the box.

1. memorize _b_
2. react ___
3. techniques ___
4. visualize ___
5. mental ___
6. landmark ___
7. portion ___
8. retain ___
9. cell ___
10. recalling ___

C 💬 Discuss these questions with a partner. Do you think you would pass "The Knowledge" test? What would you do to learn all the streets of London?

Gerunds as subjects and after prepositions

A gerund is a noun formed from a verb + *ing*.	ask → *asking* sit → *sitting* try → *trying*
Gerunds can be used as the subject of a sentence.	**Saying** new vocabulary words is a good way to remember them. **Learning** English is important for my future.
Gerunds can be used after a preposition.	I'm interested <u>in</u> **becoming** a taxi driver. We talked <u>about</u> **studying** together. He's afraid <u>of</u> **flying** on airplanes.

Engage!

What was the most difficult exam you have ever taken? How did you prepare for it?

A Complete each sentence with the gerund form of a verb from the box.

> study   do   travel   learn   forget   lose

1. He's tired of _____ for the taxi driver's exam.
2. Jackie is interested in _____ to China to learn about Chinese history.
3. I worry about _____ information from professors' lectures. What if I can't remember it when I take the exam?
4. For many people, _____ with their eyes, or visual learning, is the best way to remember things.
5. _____ something physical, like making something with one's hands, can be a good way to learn.
6. I'm afraid of _____ my wallet, so I always keep it in the same place.

B Tell your partner about good ways to do these things. Use gerunds.

> remember birthdays   practice listening to English   get more exercise

Word Focus

Other common combinations of verb + preposition:

> worry about
> look forward to
> plan on
> be tired of
> think about

> Walking to school is a good way to get more exercise.

> You could learn a new grammar structure by practicing it a lot.

Conversation

A 🔊 2 Listen to the conversation and choose the correct answer.

1. a. an important business meeting   b. her laptop
2. a. making a list   b. bringing keys when going out.

B 🔊 2 Listen to the conversation again and fill in the blanks.

Katie: Hi, Diane. You don't look very happy.
Diane: I'm not. _____, and I completely forgot to bring my laptop. My boss was really upset.
Katie: _____. You shouldn't worry about it.
Diane: _____!
Katie: Making a list is a good way of remembering things. _____.
Diane: But I'll just forget about the list!
Katie: _____. That's what I always do.

C Practice the conversation with a partner. Then make new conversations about important things you need to remember and good ways to remember them.

D GOAL CHECK ✓ **Talk about learning strategies**

Discuss the learning strategies in the box. How could you use each strategy to remember new vocabulary or other things that you need to memorize?

> taking notes
> making lists
> concentrating/paying attention
> asking questions/participating
> visualizing practicing

Unit 7 The Mind 99

B GOAL 2: Talk About Your Senses

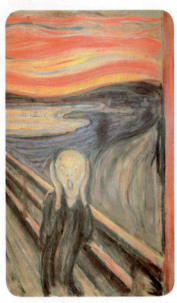

▲ *The Scream* by Edvard Munch, who had synesthesia

Listening

A Discuss the questions with a partner.

1. What's your favorite song? Why do you like it?
2. When you listen to the song, does it make you think of any of these things?

> a person   a color   an experience   a place   a season   a picture

B 3 Listen to a radio program about an unusual brain condition called *synesthesia*. Circle the answers.

1. When a person has synesthesia, two kinds of (memories | senses) work together.
2. Lori Blackman is unusual because she always sees (letters | sounds) in different colors.

SYNESTHESIA

C 3 Listen again. Circle **T** for *true* and **F** for *false*.

1. The word *synesthesia* comes from the Greek words for *together* and *senses*.   T   F
2. There are two different kinds of synesthesia.   T   F
3. Lori's father has synesthesia, too.   T   F
4. Some artists and musicians have synesthesia.   T   F
5. Lori has a lot of problems because of synesthesia.   T   F

D 3 Listen again and fill in the blanks.

1. The most common kind is called _____ synesthesia.
2. Lori realized she was unusual when she was _____ years old.
3. For Lori, the letter B is light _____.
4. About one person in _____ has synesthesia.

E Discuss the questions with a partner.

1. Do you know someone who has had experiences like this?
2. Would you like to have synesthesia? If so, what kind? If not, why not?

Pronunciation: Th sounds

A 🔊 4 *Th* has two pronunciations in English—voiced /ð/ and unvoiced /θ/. Listen and repeat the words, and notice the pronunciations of *th*.

Voiced /ð/	Unvoiced /θ/
the	think
this	three
that	theater

B Take turns saying the words. Decide which *th* sounds are voiced /ð/ and which are unvoiced /θ/.

> thousand   those   Thursday   they   thank   thief   thirsty   them

C Read the sentence below. Which words have voiced /ð/? Which words have unvoiced /θ/? Say the sentence out loud as fast as you can.

I thanked that thin thief for the three theater tickets.

Communication

A Look at the pictures on the page. Imagine you are in these situations. What can you see, hear, smell, taste, and feel? Describe as many details as you can. Use your imagination!

B **GOAL CHECK** ✓ **Talk about your senses**

Work with a partner. Imagine you are in your favorite place in the world. What can you see, hear, smell, taste, touch, and feel right now?

> I feel warm sand under my feet. I smell the ocean.

C GOAL 3: Talk About Your Fears

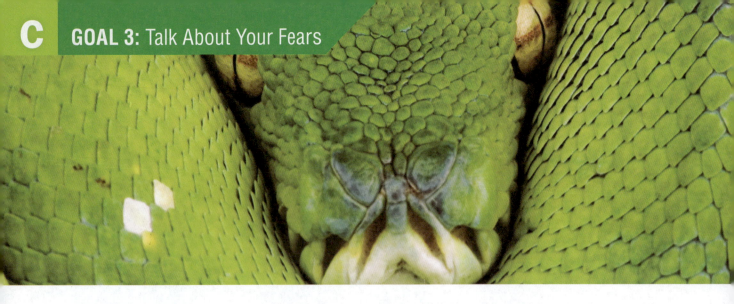

laboratory—a place where scientists work

research—studying something to discover new facts

theory—a scientific idea

survey—collecting the same information from people

experiment—a scientific test to see if something is true

results—the information that scientists get after an experiment

conduct—organize and carry out

conclusion—something you decide after looking at all the information

Language Expansion: Scientific studies

A Study the words in the box about science and their meanings.

B 🔊 5 Listen to the passage and fill in the blanks.

1. In one _____, 51 percent of people said that snakes are their biggest fear. One _____ says that fear is built into our brain. But _____ shows we might also learn to be afraid of things.

2. Scientists _____ an interesting experiment with monkeys born in a _____ at a university.

3. The lab monkeys didn't react when they were shown _____, but they became afraid when they were shown videos of wild monkeys _____. However, when they were shown a new video where the wild monkeys _____, they did not develop a fear of flower.

4. _____ show that monkeys can learn some of their fear by watching other monkeys, and the researchers' _____ was that fear is partly built into monkey's brains, but can also be learned.

C Discuss these questions with a partner. Are you afraid of snakes? Why or why not? Are you afraid of any other animals? Give your reasons.

May, might, and *could* for possibility

Use *may, might,* and *could* + base verb to say that something is possible, now or in the future.	We **may find** dangerous animals in the jungle. Monkeys **might learn** to be afraid of things. People **could develop** a fear of snakes.
Use *may, might,* and *could* to express that we are not completely sure about something.	Scientists say that other fears **are** learned. (The scientists are sure about this.) Scientists say that other fears **might be** learned. (The scientists are not sure about this, but it's possible.)

102 新世界交互英语视听说 学生用书 3

A Why are these people afraid? Complete each sentence with *may*, *might*, or *could* and a phrase from the box.

1. I don't like to walk across high bridges because ____I could fall off.____
2. Jose Luis is afraid of speaking English because _____
3. My grandmother gets nervous when she's driving because _____
4. I don't like camping because _____
5. Nancy never takes the subway because _____
6. I worry about going to the dentist because _____

> get on the wrong train
> see a snake
> have an accident
> need a filling in my tooth
> fall off
> make a mistake

B What are you afraid of? Tell your partner, and give your reasons with *may*, *might*, or *could*.

Conversation

A 🔊 6 Listen to a conversation and answer the following questions.

1. What is Andy afraid of?
   _____
2. How did Susan get over the fear?
   _____

B 🔊 6 Listen to the conversation again and fill in the blanks.

Susan: You look really nervous, Andy. What's up?
Andy: Oh, _____. I hate flying!
Susan: Really? But you travel a lot!
Andy: _____. The plane might fly into bad weather, or the pilot could make a mistake.
Susan: _____, but I got over it.
Andy: Really? How?
Susan: _____.

C Practice the conversation in Exercise **B** with a partner. Then make new conversations using the list below. Use your own ideas for ways to get over these fears.

> swimming in deep water   being in high places
> speaking in front of the class visiting the doctor/dentist

D ✓ **GOAL CHECK** **Talk about your fears**

Tell your partner about something you're afraid of. Why are you afraid of it?

Real Language

When you *get over* a bad experience or an illness, you recover from it.

Wooden stairs descending into cave

Unit 7 The Mind 103

D GOAL 4: Describe an Emotional Experience

Listening

A Discuss the questions with a partner.

1. What happened to the person in the photo? Why does he feel like this?
2. What other emotions are there?

B 7 Listen to the passage and choose the correct answer.

1. a. how people show their feelings
   b. how people in different places show their feelings
   c. how people's faces show their feelings
   d. how the Fore people show their feelings

2. a. They cannot understand the photographs of Americans.
   b. They had never seen foreign faces before.
   c. They can easily understand English.
   d. They live in the jungle in New Guinea.

3. a. The results of the experiment are similar to those he got from the previous one.
   b. The results of the experiment are contrary to those he got from the previous one.
   c. In the experiment he showed pictures of the Fore to people in other countries.
   d. In the experiment he showed pictures of Americans to the Fore.

4. a. because they are the same everywhere
   b. because they are built into our brains
   c. because they are developed to help us deal with things quickly
   d. because all of them are negative emotions which might hurt us

5. a. Paul Ekman studied people's faces in different cultures.
   b. Two people might feel different emotions about the same thing.
   c. Fear is the most difficult emotion to change.
   d. Most emotional triggers are learned.

C 🔊 7 Listen to the passage again and fill in the blanks.

1. According to Ekman, the six universal emotions are anger, _____, sadness, _____, _____, and surprise.

2. Ekman's research gave powerful support to the theory that _____ _____.

3. People might have different feelings when smelling newly-cut grass because _____.

> **Engage!**
> Do you have similar experience? Share it with your partner.

Communication

A Think about a time when you felt one of the emotions in the box. Tell your partner about your experience. Your partner will ask you for more details.

1. What happened?
2. How did you feel?
3. What did you do?
4. What did you learn from the experience?

> happiness fear
> surprise sadness
> anger   disgust

B Group work. Conduct surveys among your classmates about what makes people feel an emotion such as annoyance, curiosity, envy or gratitude. Present your findings to the class.

C | GOAL CHECK ✓ **Describe an emotional experience**

Write each emotion from the box in Exercise **A** on a small piece of paper. Mix up the pieces and place them facedown. Take turns choosing a piece of paper and talking about a time when you had that emotion. The first pair of students to finish talking about all six emotions wins.

> **Word Focus**
> You can use a variety of verbs to describe experiences.
> observe
> notice
> sense
> perceive
> imagine
> become aware of

E VIDEO JOURNAL: *Memory Man*

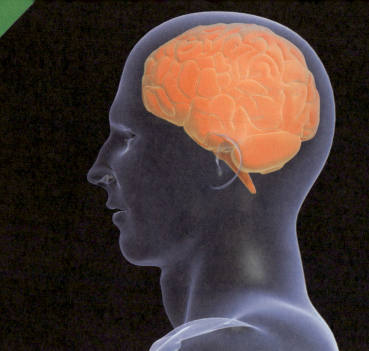

How does memory work?

When we get new information, it goes into a part of the brain called the **hippocampus**. There the information is **coded** and put into memory. But why are some people better at remembering? Some scientists think a good memory comes from **heredity**. We get it from our parents through their **genes**. Other people say a good memory comes from practice.

Before You Watch

A Read the information in the box and study the words in **bold**.

While You Watch

A ▶ Watch the video. Complete the sentences.

1. Gianni Golfera is blindfolded, but he can still do something that's _____ _____.
2. He has memorized more than _____ books.
3. Researchers are studying how memory and _____ change the brain.
4. For Gianni, improving his memory has become a _____.
5. Gianni's life is not all about _____, though.
6. Gianni's practice is making his memory _____.

After You Watch/Communication

A Discuss these questions with a partner. Why do you think Gianni Golfera has such a good memory? Would you like to take Gianni's memory class? Give your reasons.

B Follow the steps to play a famous memory game.

1. Choose twelve small objects. Put them on top of a desk and cover them.
2. Change places with another student. In one minute, try to memorize the objects you see on that student's desk.
3. List all the objects you can remember in two minutes. Check your lists. Who remembered the most objects?

Further Practice: The Mind-Body Connection   F

Listening

A 🔊 8 Listen to the passage. Circle **T** for *true*, **F** for *false*, or **NI** for *no information* (if the answer is not in the listening).

1. Norman Cousins became ill while he was traveling in another country. **T F NI**
2. Doctors told Cousins that he would probably die from his disease. **T F NI**
3. Drugs helped to stop the pain of Cousins's disease. **T F NI**
4. Cousins started watching movies because he was bored. **T F NI**
5. Cousins spent a lot of time laughing every day. **T F NI**
6. Movies were better than funny stories for stopping pain. **T F NI**
7. When Cousins wrote his book, everyone agreed with him. **T F NI**
8. Scientists have done research on using laughter to stop pain. **T F NI**

B 🔊 8 Number the events in order.

___ Cousins watched funny movies and cartoons all day.
___ Cousins went back to work.
___ Cousins went to a hospital.
___ Doctors told Cousins he had a terrible disease.
___ Researchers found that Cousins's ideas were right.
___ Cousins took many medications.
___ The pain didn't get better.
___ People didn't agree with Cousins's ideas.
___ Cousins felt much better.

▲ Norman Cousins

C Can your mind make your body sick or well? Take notes then talk about your opinion. Give reasons and explanations.

_____
_____
_____
_____
_____

UNIT 8
Changing Planet

Buried air and gas from bacteria and algae bubble to the ice's surface in Greenland.

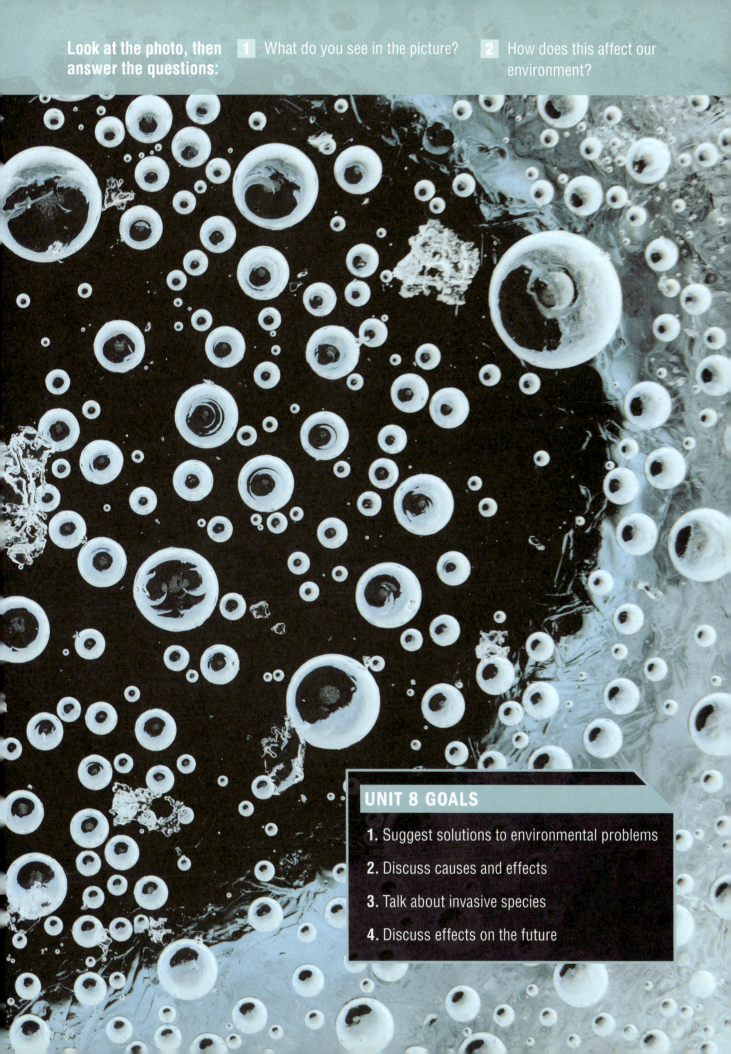

Look at the photo, then answer the questions:

1 What do you see in the picture?

2 How does this affect our environment?

UNIT 8 GOALS

1. Suggest solutions to environmental problems

2. Discuss causes and effects

3. Talk about invasive species

4. Discuss effects on the future

A GOAL 1: Suggest Solutions to Environmental Problems

▲ Access roads and terraced fields in Sarawak, Borneo, Malaysia

Vocabulary

A Match the words in the left column with their meanings in the right column.

1. polar
2. extreme
3. deforestation
4. drought
5. conservation
6. increase
7. global warming
8. sea levels
9. lead to
10. climate change

a. the cutting down of forests
b. rise in Earth's temperature
c. cause, result in
d. protecting the environment
e. connected with, or near the North or South Pole
f. a period with much less rain
g. very great in degree or intensity
h. a change in weather patterns
i. the average water levels
j. amount becoming greater

B 🔊 1 Listen to the passage and match the causes and its effects.

Causes

1. global travel
2. use of coal and oil
3. demand for tree products and farmland
4. global warming

Effects

a. deforestation
b. invasive species
c. global warming
d. less polar ice

Conversation

A 🔊 2 Listen to the conversation and answer the following questions.

1. What does Pedro think should be done about climate change?

   _____
   _____
   _____

2. What can trees do to help reduce the effects of climate change according to Pedro?

   _____
   _____
   _____

B 🔊 2 Listen to the conversation again and fill in the blanks. Check your answers with your partner's.

Sonia: Hey, what's up? _____.

Pedro: I am worried.

Sonia: About what?

Pedro: I hear a lot about climate change, but I _____
_____.

Sonia: I know what you mean, but what do you think should be done?

Pedro: Well, _____. More trees could be planted.

Sonia: Would that help?

Pedro: Definitely! _____, so they don't become heat islands.

Sonia: Heat islands! I learn something new every day.

C Practice the conversation with a partner. Make new conversations with your own ideas for solving the climate change problem.

D Discuss how climate change is affecting China. Make a list of things that are being done about it (or that could be done).

E **GOAL CHECK** ✓ **Suggest solutions to environmental problems**

Share your group's list from Exercise **D** with the class.

> Laws have been passed to reduce pollution from cars.

> Right. We can only drive on certain days of the week.

B GOAL 2: Discuss Causes and Effects

1. _____

2. _____

3. _____

4. _____

Listening

A Rank these types of extreme weather from most serious (1) to least serious (5) in your opinion. Then compare your rankings with your partner's.

____ floods

____ very cold weather

____ hurricanes/typhoons

____ drought

____ very hot weather

B 🔊 3 Listen to four people talking about climate change. Write the name of a place below each picture on the left.

C 🔊 3 Listen again. Answer the questions.

1. According to Mari, what is happening to the cattle?
2. How many deaths occurred in Europe during one heat wave?
3. Why do some scientists say that global warming isn't causing the heat waves?
4. According to Joseph, how many hurricanes and tropical storms occurred one year?
5. How does warm ocean water cause strong storms?
6. How are recent floods in Jasmine's country different than in the past?

Pronunciation: Linking words together

When a word ends in a consonant sound and the next word begins with a vowel sound, the words are linked together.

What's the capital of Japan? (Can you hear the word *of*?)

When a word ends in a consonant sound and the next word begins with the same consonant sound, the words are linked and the sound is only pronounced once.

We didn't feel like going home, so we went to the museum. (Can you hear *fee-like* and *wen-to*?)

A 4 Underline the sounds that link together. Then listen and check your answers.

1. Climate change has been in the news lately.
2. We've received dozens of letters.
3. Will this rain never end?
4. The heat takes a toll on the human body.
5. The governor is worried about food shortages.
6. Is that a good way to save energy?

B Write sentences using these word pairs in your notebook. Then practice saying the sentences with a partner.

1. weather report
2. gone over
3. above average
4. coldest temperatures
5. drought ended
6. more rainfall

Communication

A How do these things happen? Talk about the causes with your partner.

1. rising sea levels
2. invasive species
3. pollution in the atmosphere
4. fewer trees
5. more extreme weather

> Air pollution is caused by burning coal and oil.

> Yes, and air pollution causes an increase in temperatures.

B Compare answers with another pair. Does everyone agree?

C **GOAL CHECK** ✓ **Discuss causes and effects**

Make a list of things you do every day that affect the environment. Then explain your list to the class.

GOAL 3: Talk About Invasive Species

Language Expansion: Large numbers

Saying large numbers	
To say large numbers in English, start at the left, and say the numbers in groups:	
hundreds (100s)	524 → five hundred (and) twenty-four
thousands (1,000s)	1,250 → one thousand, two hundred (and) fifty
ten thousands (10,000s)	17,400 → seventeen thousand (and) four hundred
hundred thousands (100,000s)	432,060 → four hundred thirty-two thousand (and) sixty
millions (1,000,000s)	2,400,900 → two million, four hundred thousand (and) nine hundred

A 🔊 5 Listen to five large numbers and write them down.

1. _____
2. _____
3. _____
4. _____
5. _____

B Discuss the questions with a partner.

1. What are invasive species? Can you think of an example?
2. Why are invasive species a problem?

▲ Leaf beetle

C Read about Macquarie Island. Guess which number is correct.

Like many places, Macquarie Island has invasive species—species of nonnative plants and animals with no local natural controls on their populations. First came the cats, which were used on ships to control rats. Then came the rabbits, which were brought by seal hunters as a source of food. The hunters came because Macquarie Island is visited by around **(8,000/80,000/800,000)** elephant seals each year. No hunting is allowed now, however, because the island is a wildlife sanctuary.

Macquarie Island has also been an accidental sanctuary for its invasive species. The rabbits found plenty to eat, and they ate an enormous amount of the island's plant life. In 1968, scientists wanted to decrease the rabbit population, so the European rabbit flea (which carries a virus called myxomatosis) was introduced. By the 1980s, the rabbit population had declined from **(1,300/13,000/130,000)** to only **(2,000/20,000/200,000)**, and the vegetation on the island had begun to recover. But with fewer rabbits to eat, the cats began to prey on the island's sea birds, so scientists decided to kill the island's cats.

Problem solved? Unfortunately, the virus had only reduced the rabbit population, and with the cats gone, the rabbits' numbers increased again. Now that so much of the island's vegetation is gone, there have been landslides after heavy rains. One expert estimates that it will cost **($162,000/$1,620,000/$16,200,000)** to finally solve the invasive species problem on Macquarie Island.

D 🔊 6 Listen and check your answers.

▲ Royal penguins returning to their colony in Macquarie Island, Australia

Conversation

A 🔊 7 Listen to the conversation and choose the correct answer.

1. a. a ship   b. a kind of insect
   c. a carrot   d. a box of food
2. a. They will kill the insect.   b. They know what the insect is.
   c. They have seen one before.   d. They will report to the biology teacher.

B 🔊 7 Listen to the conversation again and fill in the blanks. Check your answers with your partner.

Abdullah: Look at this, Henry.

Henry: Eeeew... What is it?

Abdullah: I'm not sure. It's _____, but I've never seen one like it.

Henry: Maybe it came here on a ship—in a box of food.

Abdullah: Right! The ship had probably been to another country to _____... carrots!

Henry: Sure. And after that, the ship came here.

Abdullah: And now our country _____ the terrible Carrot Beetle!

Henry: Not if we do something about it first.

Abdullah: _____, Henry. We can't kill it if we don't even know what it is.

Henry: You're right. Maybe we should _____.

C Practice the conversation. Make new conversations about invasive species in your city with a partner.

D | GOAL CHECK ✓ | **Talk about invasive species**

With a partner, discuss the events on Macquarie Island in your own words. What had the island been like before people arrived? What problem did each new species cause?

Unit 8 Changing Planet 115

D GOAL 4: Discuss Effects on the Future

Listening

A Check (✓) the actions in the list that can affect our future. Share your ideas with a partner.

_____ 1. If everyone drives their own car, we might run out of fuel.

_____ 2. If we use energy-efficient light bulbs, we will use less electricity.

_____ 3. If the world's population keeps growing, we might not have enough food and water.

_____ 4. If we protect wilderness areas, we can save endangered species.

_____ 5. If we use biofuels, we might reduce CO_2 emissions.

B 8 Listen to the passage. Match the actions with the results. Compare your answers with your partner's.

_____ 1. make small changes in how we use energy

_____ 2. use renewable biofuels

_____ 3. paint building roofs white

_____ 4. know the ecological cost of our choices

a. make decisions that are good for the future

b. save money on lighting and air conditioning

c. have a big impact on the planet

d. keep tons of CO_2 out of the air

C 8 Listen again. Complete the sentences.

1. John Doerr's main job is in finance, but he is also interested in _____.

2. A compact fluorescent light bulb can last as long as _____ years.

3. In _____, 40% of vehicles use biofuels instead of gasoline.

4. According to Doerr, companies can also help the environment by changing the way they use _____.

Word Focus

impact a powerful or major influence or effect
renewable able to be replaced by nature
biofuel a material produced from plants that is burned to produce heat or power
CO_2 a gas that is produced when people and animals breathe out or when certain fuels are burned, and that is used by plants for energy: carbon dioxide
skylight a window in the roof of a house or on a ship's deck

"I really, really hope that we multiply all of our energy, all of our talent, and all of our influence to solve this problem."

John Doerr's idea worth spreading is that being green is the most important thing anyone can do. And we need to do it more—right now. Watch Doerr's full TED Talk on TED.com.

D GOAL 4: Discuss Effects on the Future

▲ CO_2 is generated when bottled water is moved from the source to the store.

Communication

A Look at the picture and answer the questions. Does drinking bottled water affect the environment? If yes, in what ways?

B Think about actions and their environmental impact that can affect the future. Rank them from most positive to most negative. Share your ideas with a partner.

____ If everyone drives their own car, we might run out of fuel.

____ If we use energy-efficient light bulbs, we will use less electricity.

____ If the world's population keeps growing, we might not have enough food and water.

____ If we protect wilderness areas, we can save endangered species.

____ If we use biofuels, we might reduce CO_2 emissions.

C GOAL CHECK ✓ Discuss Effects on the Future

Share your rankings of actions that affect the future. Brainstorm two more positive and negative actions. Who is responsible for these actions? Doerr mentions individuals, businesses, and governments. What could each group do about these actions?

VIDEO JOURNAL: *The Netherlands: Rising Water* E

A canal in Amsterdam

Before You Watch

A Read some quick facts about the Netherlands.

- Another name for the Netherlands is Holland.
- About half of the country's land is below sea level.
- The Dutch have built walls called *dikes* between the sea and the land. They have created new areas of dry land.
- Windmills move water to the sea, and as the water is removed, the land **sinks** even lower.
- As sea levels **rise** due to global warming, the Dutch must decide how to deal with the rising water. Should they continue to **struggle** against the sea?

While You Watch

A ▶ Watch the video and choose the best phrase to complete each sentence.

1. Instead of fighting the sea, it might be necessary to _____.
   a. struggle against the sea
   b. give land back to the sea

2. Flood control lakes could be used for _____.
   a. recreation and wildlife
   b. farmland

3. Older Dutch people don't like the idea because they think _____.
   a. fighting the water is necessary
   b. water makes a pretty landscape

After You Watch/Communication

A What are the advantages of letting some of the land in the Netherlands fill up with water? What are the disadvantages?

Unit 8 Changing Planet 119

F Further Practice: *What Can One City Do?*

Listening

A Have a discussion with your partner about what could be done in your school to help the environment? Complete the chart with your ideas.

teaching people about the environment	1.
	2.
electricity and energy	1.
	2.
garbage	1.
	2.
using less paper	1.
	2.

B 🔊 9 Listen to the passage and choose the correct answer.

1. Naema Omar is trying to save energy for _____.
   a. heat   b. lighting   c. both **a** and **b**
2. One problem with saving energy is that _____.
   a. it isn't always successful
   b. you need money
   c. you can't do it in old houses
3. The Cambridge Energy Alliance is working to save energy in _____.
   a. buildings   b. cars   c. both **a** and **b**
4. If people need money to do home energy projects, _____ helps them get it.
   a. their bank   b. the CEA   c. the government
5. The city of Cambridge wants to _____.
   a. stop new houses from producing carbon dioxide
   b. help other cities save energy
   c. make efficient new houses
6. Saving energy can _____.
   a. save money for people   b. make new jobs   c. both **a** and **b**

C 🔊 9 Listen again. Number these steps in order.
_____ The Cambridge Energy Alliance makes a plan for the home.
__1__ People want to save energy in their homes.
_____ People contact the Cambridge Energy Alliance.
_____ People use the money to make energy improvements in their homes.
_____ The Cambridge Energy Alliance goes to the home.
_____ People pay back the loan with the money they save on energy.
_____ The Cambridge Energy Alliance helps people get money.

D Talk about three things that people in China can do to save energy and why should they do these things?

Sylvia Earle Oceanographer, National Geographic Explorer-in-Residence

MY WISH—PROTECT OUR OCEANS

Before You Watch

Sylvia Earle's idea worth spreading is that we need to do a better job of looking after our oceans, the world's "life support system." Watch Earle's full **TED**Talk on TED.com.

A Look at the picture and answer the questions with a partner.

1. Where are these people?
2. Why are they there?
3. What do you think they're doing?

B Sylvia Earle is one of the explorers in the picture. Here are some words you will hear in her TED Talk. Complete the paragraph with the correct word. Not all words will be used.

> **assets** *n.* valuable people or things
> **cope** *v.* to deal with problems and difficult situations and try to come up with solutions
> **depletion** *n.* reduction, shortage
> **drawn down** *v.* reduced
> **enduring** *adj.* continuing to exist in the same state or condition
> **impact** *n.* a powerful or major influence or effect
> **resilient** *adj.* able to become strong, healthy, or successful again after something bad happens

She is worried about the _____ of sea life she has seen—90% of the world's big fish are gone, _____ by a growing population, pollution, and wasteful fishing practices. Dr. Earle believes that we must all work together to _____ with this problem by reducing our _____ on the ocean before it is too late.

C Look at the pictures on the next page. Check (✓) the information that you predict you will hear in the TED Talk.

____ 1. The deep ocean is a dangerous place for humans.
____ 2. When we know more about creatures that live in the sea, we can protect them better.
____ 3. Human activity has changed the ocean in many negative ways.

While You Watch

A Watch the TED Talk. Circle the main idea.

1. If we don't protect the ocean, humans will be in danger, too.
2. There are many kinds of fish in the ocean that we don't know about.
3. It is important to develop new ways to catch fish.

Dr. Sylvia Earle has been exploring Earth's oceans for more than 50 years. She knows how important it is to protect the _____ that are found in the sea.

" ... Nothing else will matter if we fail to protect the ocean. Our fate and the ocean's are one."

—Sylvia Earle

B ▶ Look at the photos. Watch the TED Talk again and write the letter of the caption under the correct photo.

a. Sylvia Earle has developed many devices for underwater exploration.

b. There are many amazing creatures in the ocean.

c. Polar ice is shrinking, and life for polar bears is getting harder.

d. Sylvia Earle loves the ocean and all the creatures that live in it.

1. ___

2. ___

3. ___

4. ___

Challenge! How would you describe Dr. Sylvia Earle's work as an ocean explorer? Is her work difficult or easy? Why does she do it? Talk to a partner about Sylvia Earle's career.

Sylvia Earle Oceanographer, National Geographic Explorer-in-Residence

MY WISH—PROTECT OUR OCEANS

After You Watch

A Complete the summary with the words in the box.

Sylvia Earle is worried about the _____. Even more, she is worried about our planet's _____. The ocean is our life _____ system, and if we don't protect it, we will be in _____. Dr. Earle wants us to _____ the ocean and its creatures better, because if we understand the seas better, we will want to _____ them.

ocean	protect
support	survival
trouble	understand

B Match the phrases to the information from the TED Talk.

_____ 1. percent of the world's oceans that is protected   **a.** 50

_____ 2. years that Sylvia Earle has been exploring the ocean   **b.** 90

_____ 3. percent of life on the planet that lives in the ocean   **c.** 10

_____ 4. percent of large fish species that have disappeared   **d.** 97

_____ 5. number of years we have to protect the ocean   **e.** 08

C Read the statements below. Circle the ones that paraphrase Sylvia Earle's ideas in the video.

1. The loss of fish species in the last 50 years is a problem.
2. People should use the ocean's resources any way they want to.
3. The oceans make it possible for human beings to live on earth.
4. The creatures that live in the deep ocean aren't as important as those on land.
5. We only have a short time to protect the ocean.

One reason for the depletion of ocean resources is wasteful fishing practices.

Project

Sylvia Earle says that if we don't work to protect the oceans right now, we risk all life on the planet. She works with other scientists and explorers to find ways to protect and sustain ocean environments. What can be done to keep the ocean healthy for future generations?

A Look at these ways we can work to protect the ocean. Which ones are the most urgent? Rank them from most urgent (1) to less urgent (6).

_____ recycle plastics so they don't end up in the ocean

_____ change the way fishermen work so that less fish is wasted

_____ keep oil and other toxic chemicals out of the sea

_____ use less energy (gasoline and electricity) to slow global warming

_____ share the message that protecting the ocean is our collective responsibility

_____ establish conservation/protection zones

B Compare your rankings in Exercise **A** with a partner. Do you have the same priorities? Think of some other ways to protect the ocean.

C Use Sylvia Earle's ideas to write a paragraph about ways we can help keep the ocean safe for future generations. Then show your paragraph to a different partner. Are your ideas well organized?

> The oceans are in danger, and everyone can help to save them. If we want to _____, we should start with _____.
> By doing _____, we can. It is also important to change _____. Finally, we need to _____.

Research Strategy

Using the search function on web pages

If you want to learn more about a topic on a Web site, use the Web site's search function. You can usually find search windows at the top of the page. They are usually located next to a magnifying glass icon. Sometimes search results can be sorted by relevance, date of publication, or type of resource.

Challenge! Dr. Sylvia Earle, a TED prize winner, has a really big idea worth spreading—one that can change the world and save our oceans. Research what China's experts are doing to protect oceans and other aquatic environments. Share your ideas with the class.